All You Need to Know about Teaching

Better communication in class and what it rests upon

Fabian Rieser

All You Need to Know About Teaching
Copyright © 2021 Fabian Rieser
www.fabianrieser.com

Author photo: Günther Bauer **www.guentherbauer.de**
Book design and layout: Sadie Butterworth-Jones
Editing: Maureen Hochdorf
Illustrations: Valentina "Vanya3"

Paperback ISBN 978-3-00-066783-1
eBook ISBN 978-3-00-066784-8

Dedicated to my secret co-author:

Valentina

Contents

Acknowledgements

This book is dedicated to my father and my brother, acknowledging their great positive influence on my life, both in good times and in difficult ones.

Writing this book has been a long process. I am especially indebted to my students for many long and interesting discussions. There is nothing in the world as good as keeping your wits sharp as a room full of bright young people criticize, argue, and help you get better!

I would like to offer my sincere thanks, especially to Giacomo Mura and Bernadette Fisher, for reading the manuscript and offering benevolent criticism. They made this the better book.

Also, I am indebted to HR Dr. Herbert Faymann for invaluable input and many fruitful discussions over the years, contributing greatly to my personal as well as professional development.

I wish to thank Sadie (formatting).

I wish to thank Maureen (editing).

I wish to thank Valentina "Vanya3" (on Fiverr) for providing the illustrations, Günther Bauer for taking my photo.

I wish to thank Hessische Kulturstiftung for generously funding this project.

I wish to thank Raphael Fuchs, Marie-Christine Pape and Diana Krähling for giving their support (each in their individual ways). Thank you very much!

Frankfurt/Main, Spring 2021
Fabian Rieser

Foreword

Dear colleagues,

I've been teaching for more than twenty years now: I'm a musician, a violinist, and I have been teaching violin since I was a student myself. I also teach teachers.

For a few years now, I've been training future teachers at the conservatory. I see that as a great privilege! Teaching the next generation is wonderful. It's a great opportunity and also a great responsibility.

This feeling of responsibility has led to a lot of self-scrutiny on my part.

Sometimes I joke with my students, saying that I would like to apologize to all of them (let's say) in the first five years of my teaching. I must have been awful!

As jokes go, I'm (of course) kidding. But there's also truth in it.

When I started, I honestly had very little clue of what I was doing. I'm absolutely certain: Teaching is one of the *most demanding jobs* there is. Looking back, I think I was ill-prepared.

My own teaching experience started with one-on-one settings — as is most common (for historical reasons) when teaching and learning a classical instrument. Later, I also began teaching groups and giving seminars. But the *intensity and directness* of personalized teaching shaped my whole outlook on education.

I firmly believe that the individual relationship between teacher and student method is key for educational success. This individual relationship is easily apparent in one-on-one teaching settings. In groups, it's much less evident. Nevertheless, we can also try to forge educational relationships of this kind when addressing groups.

This book is me trying to write down the most important things I learned throughout twenty years of teaching. I would like to share it all with you, hoping that you won't make the mistakes I made on this path. After all, this is how we achieve progress - by building on each other's experiences and learning from them.

- If you are starting a career in teaching a musical instrument right now, this book is for you.
- If you are *already* a teacher, this book is also for you.

My greatest hope is that even people outside the realm of music education, outside our small community of "teachers teaching musical instruments," will find this book useful.

I know I come from a very specialized field — teaching a musical instrument is a niche. That's true. On the other hand, learning is a *basic aspect* of being human. So at the core, teaching the violin and teaching (let's say) yoga or painting or (fill in the blank) actually have quite a lot in common!

We understand new things based on what we already know. So, the brain tends to frame new things *in reference* to past experiences. This is why it is sometimes so hard to gain new viewpoints.

Seeing things differently is demanding — it requires effort. Changing our perspective doesn't come naturally to us. It is a *challenge*. We tend to reject new information if it goes against our established belief systems. We subconsciously try to protect our sense of self and that by being resistant to new information and changing our behavior.

Therefore, the core theme of this book is: *Learning is tricky!*

Books are like long letters to friends. I try to lay out my argument here in this book, taking you on a journey — a journey through my way of thinking. You may find some of the stuff in this book great. Some you may have heard already numerous times, and some you may disagree with. Some may be just boring for you. All of that is okay!

Also, I must admit, the title, "All You Need to Know About Teaching," is misleading. It's tongue in cheek. What an outrage! We haven't even started our journey together yet, and already I'm misleading you!

The truth of the matter is, teaching is an *art*. As arts go, it's *limitless*. I wouldn't presume to know nearly as much about it as I would wish to, but what I know, I will share with you. None of this is new. It's the stuff I've learned from many sources over the years (the sources are in the endnotes). Some of it has been known for centuries or, in the case of non-violent communication, even millennia.

My overall goal is to reduce suffering in education. (And believe me, there is a lot of suffering in education.) I like to quote Antoine de Saint-Exupéry, "A goal without a plan is just a wish." This book is my plan to bring us all closer to the goal because wishful thinking alone will accomplish nothing.

This book is an invitation, nothing more.

So, please feel invited.

PART 1

I'm a teacher, and my background is in music. Teaching music is somewhat special. Playing a musical instrument is an art, and teaching a musical instrument is also an art, but this specialness is built on a common basis. It's built on the basis of how teaching works in general.

I'm absolutely certain that teaching music is not fundamentally different from teaching (let's say) drawing, sports or math. The act of teaching rests on fundamental principles, for example, the brain's ability to reshape itself, our ability to memorize, and the way we can understand human behavior through interaction (just to name a few).

- **Part 1** will look into personal matters: Our beliefs, our basic needs, attachment, and personal growth. The idea behind this approach is that the better we know ourselves, the better we can help others.
- **Part 2** will dive into aspects of cognitive science, emotion psychology, and stress. All this will, in turn, be the foundation for part three.
- **Part 3** I will talk about my personal take-aways from all this, my personal tool kit for teaching. I explain the basic concepts of empathy, validation, and acceptance. You will also receive sentences and questions at hand, ready for direct use in your teaching.

Chapter 1
What is this all about?

When I started teaching, I was amazed to see that many musicians who are great at playing their instruments are quite *bad teachers*. That may be surprising at first but think about it - teaching is absolutely not the same thing as playing. It requires a radically different skill set than standing on stage or recording in a studio. The point is that when great musicians start to teach, they tend to fail at being good teachers.

This is normally the case because they teach in the manner in which they were taught themselves. Their own understanding of music and how to progress determines how they teach. Typically, they don't think about this - they simply try (in good faith) to help others follow their own path. Their mistake is to believe that others can easily do that.

Nothing could be further from the truth.

Teaching something is very different from being able to do something. That's why great experts tend to be bad teachers. Maybe, in a few lucky cases, their teachings work.

Mostly, they don't.

If you want to check, the internet gives us access to a lot of great performers sharing their thoughts on practicing, technical difficulties, teaching, and life in general. Lots of instructional videos are available online.

Sometimes, these videos are great. Sometimes, these videos are not great *at all*. And sometimes, you can see that what the artist is doing and what he or she tells you about it are two totally different things!

It's funny because (I'm absolutely sure) there is no malice behind it. It simply has to do with self —awareness. Let's be honest; I believe these great artists never encountered the technical problems of "normal" people. If you meet them (and I have met some), the most astonishing fact is that the hardest stuff seems so easy for them.

They may be, in all honesty, telling what they believe they are doing. But if you look closer and analyze it, you see that there's much more going on. I know I may be harming my own case here, but if you have the choice, *look closely* and try to understand what this person is *doing*. Don't listen too much to what they say.

Or at least, take it with a grain of salt. In my own life, my development was sometimes greatly hampered by following well-meant but ultimately *bad* advice.

Of course, not all videos are bad. There are actually many good ones. The tricky part is to sort through them and find that specific piece of information beneficial to you.

I would like to give you some help in this regard. I will show you how learning works, the processes behind it, and how you can learn effectively. This way, your progress will be much faster, whatever your field.

# Important points to remember

✓   Having a skill and teaching it are two different things.

✓   Teaching is based on fundamental principles of human cognition and interaction.

✓   Successful teaching needs different skills and knowledge than the craft being taught.

Chapter 2

Learning & Memory

I started by saying that teaching rests on fundamental principles. So, the first question, which comes to mind, is:

What is learning?

Learning means quite simply that you acquire something (a skill, a thought, whatever), which you didn't have before. We do that *all the time*. Some people say that the only thing the brain cannot do is *not to learn*. I think that is true.

The way we understand learning and how the brain works dramatically changed over the last twenty years. There is a lot of exciting research in this field. One of the greatest brain researchers is Eric Kandel.[1] He won the Nobel Prize in 2000 for revolutionizing our understanding of the brain and its inner mechanisms.

In a nutshell, the brain has an absolutely amazing property: *It can change itself.*

Perhaps this does not sound exciting to you. But, can your hand change? Can you grow an extra finger or toe?

No, of course, you can't.

Your brain, however, grows and continually adapts. In neurobiology, this is called *synaptic plasticity*. Synaptic plasticity means that nerve cells in our brain can connect with other nerve cells. You cannot grow a new finger, but the neurons, the nerve cells, in your brain can grow new connections to other neurons all the time.

They do so to communicate with other cells easier.

These new connections form as a result of new experiences. They correspond or *correlate* to new experiences. If you watch a movie, read a book, or talk to a friend, your brain will have changed afterward. We remember scenes from movies (or something someone told us) because these memories are stored in our brains.

Storage in the brain is accomplished by growing a web of new connections - the nerve cells in our brain wire and rewire according to our experiences. To be precise, first, the brain works with what it already has (functional strengthening), then it grows new connections (plasticity). The more often we have an experience, or the stronger it is emotionally, the thicker the new connections become.

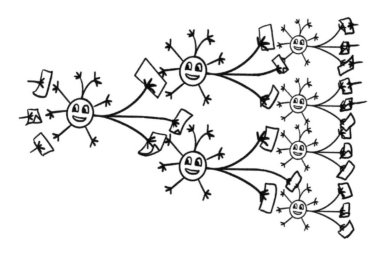

Information is passed on from neuron to neuron through electric charges.

We fall in love, we hate, we learn, and we forget — all this is due to processes in the brain. We are the way we are and who we are because of learning, memory, and the underlying process of synaptic plasticity. [2] One can say that it is our memory that allows us to have a consistent mental life.

Now comes the real clinch.

The way we *feel* directly impacts how we learn. It even affects how much we learn and if we learn at all. Smart and sensitive people have known that for ages. Now, these hunches are confirmed by objective research data. A 2017 review by Tyng et al. shows that the parts of our brain, which are concerned with emotions, have the power to switch on and off learning! They can dramatically change the ability of nerve cells to form new connections.

I'm sure you have witnessed this effect already yourself.

Imagine you have to prepare for an important exam - let's say in math. Sorry, math nerds , math was always my weakest topic in school. You are preparing and trying to learn, but also you are so immensely stressed, your brain feels numb, you just want this to be over, and nothing sticks in your memory. Sounds familiar?

Well, that's what scientists call *affective inhibition*. It means that your strong negative emotions ("OMG, math!") keep you from committing anything to your memory.[3] And it's not only happening with strong negative emotions. It also occurs if you try to learn too much in too short a time. Or too much *similar* stuff at the same time. For example, imagine there is a test coming up in French and another one in Spanish. If you learn the vocabulary for both tests side by side, you may end up mixing the two languages in your memory.

So, emotions are extremely powerful in the way they affect our memory. And we are not even speaking about *trauma* yet! When a person has severe trauma (surviving a traffic accident or something similar), the memory leading up to this highly stressful event will likely be erased. That is called *retrograde amnesia* in medicine. It can have severe long-term effects. (Thankfully, traffic accidents don't happen to us too often and are relatively rare.)

Interestingly, if you compare the stress levels alone, traffic accidents and stage performances are not so far off. That's why I chose a traffic accident as an example. Patsy Rodenburg said that "someone going on stage for press night undergoes the same stress as someone suffering a major car accident. It's a massive blow to the body in terms of the adrenaline."[4]

Even though events like plane crashes, terrorist attacks, or dangerous traffic accidents don't happen to us often (thankfully!), other experiences with similar stress levels do. These experiences may look much less threatening on the surface, but they can have a strong influence on us nevertheless. Negative emotions impact our memory a great deal. In the end, it's not the objective assessment of danger that is important, but how we feel about it subjectively.

Compared to a car accident, a math exam may not look like a big deal. But in reality, the processes in effect are quite similar. In both cases, our memory can be significantly affected by the stress level we feel. Often, it is how we feel in a situation, the importance we give it in our mind, which determines how much we will remember.

The important point is that there is no such thing as an "objective" stress level. Stress is always assessed individually. If something is stressful for you, it simply is. I can try to argue with you - why the given situation may not be stressful, why you should feel differently, what I would do in your shoes, and so on — but this argument will not help you. Most likely, you will still *feel bad* in addition to your stress.

The only beneficial strategy is to live through the stressful situation and master it. It's like looking back at high school exams. When you're older (past high school), they seem like no big deal any longer. At that time, they were momentous, right?

If you come out of a stressful situation on top, you will have gained a new frame of reference. It's powerful for the next time. It is the basis on which you will judge the next time. We must learn that we can succeed in doing so.

But can this be achieved?

Most of the time, talking is not sufficient for that. We must experience it.

I remember the time when I was a student, battling these issues. It was hard, and I decided to get help tackling them. My initial idea was, let's get a book!

So, I bought a highly recommended book from the self-help section at my local book store. I read it cover to cover in no time. I had high hopes. The book was a great read and addressed all my anxieties. The main ideas conveyed that if you control the way you think, the sky is your limit! With a positive mindset, you will get positive results easily! Just pull yourself together! Pull yourself up by your bootstraps! Be disciplined! (You know the type of book).

The book recommended self-affirmations, writing down all your strengths, and placing post-its all over your apartment (bathroom mirror, above the kitchen sink, next to your computer - you get the picture). Being a good student, I followed the advice to the letter. My apartment sure brightened up with all the colorful post-its on every available surface.

But the funny thing was that my improved room decoration was about the only positive result from my efforts. Rather than feeling more confident, I actually felt more miserable! The problem was that my wonderful affirmations didn't work.

To be precise, they not only did not work - they made me even *feel worse*. Facing failure, I berated myself. Maybe I didn't do the affirmations enough or in the right way? Perhaps I didn't deserve success? Or it just wasn't meant to be?

It was a complete and utter disaster.

Much later, a friend told me that this outcome is quite common. The problem with positive affirmations is that they focus on the conscious level of thought. Sigmund Freud already knew that the conscious part of our brain activity is very small. A popular comparison (attributed to him) likens the mind to an iceberg. The conscious mind is the tip above the water. The bulk of the *iceberg* is below the water line — the powerful subconscious.[5]

If you try to make the mind believe a positive affirmation, the subconscious checks its content. If the affirmation conflicts with a deeply ingrained negative belief, you end up in a *mighty inner fight*. Conscious and subconscious are battling it out. You can guess the outcome.

The subconscious wins most of the time.

# Important points to remember

✓   Nerve cells in our brain have the ability to connect with other nerve cells due to experiences we have (synaptic plasticity).

✓   Emotions are extremely powerful in the way they affect our memory.

✓   There is no such thing as an "objective" stress level. Stress is always assessed individually.

✓   Affirmations often do not work.

Chapter references

1   If you are interested, check out his books: https://www.indiebound.org/book/9780231179621

2   Kandel explains the process of synaptic plasticity in-depth in his 2007 book: "In Search of Memory: The Emergence of a New Science of Mind." It's a great book content-wise and also easy to read.

3   See for more information: Bäuml, Karl-Heinz/Pastötter, Bernhard/ Hanslmayr, Simon (2010): "Binding and inhibition in episodic memory-Cognitive, emotional, and neural processes." In: Neuroscience & Biobehavioral Reviews 34, 7, 1047-1054.

4   The full interview you can find here: Rodenburg, Patsy (2012): "How to develop great performing presence." The Strad 122 (5), 52-57.

5   It's not quite clear if this comparison is really by Freud. In his works, no "iceberg-model" can be found. Furthermore, his idea of the mind is quite fluid, which goes against comparing the mind with a (rather static) iceberg. Nevertheless, in Ruch, Floyd L./Zimbardo, Philip G.(1974, 366), the reference to Freud can be found.

Chapter 3
"What do I believe in?" — Beliefs and Values

We carry around all sorts of beliefs: Everybody does. You have your ideas, and — if you teach — you can safely assume that your students hold theirs, too. Beliefs are rooted in our past experiences, our family upbringing, the schools we went to, and so on. Genetics also play a role. *Our beliefs form a great deal of our identity*.

Identity and beliefs are crucial for learning. As teachers, we tend to think too little about belief systems. Learning something is challenging because it requires change. As humans, we tend to see change as a threat. We can approach new situations negatively as threats or more positively as challenges. How we approach a situation greatly depends on our acquired beliefs. In this sense, all the self-help-gurus are right. Our attitude matters!

But the problem is that we cannot easily change these belief systems - they are sometimes very old, deeply engrained, and are reinforced very often. You already know that frequently used brain pathways get stronger (plasticity), which strengthens them. So, if a belief is continually reinforced, it gains strength.

For reinforcement, it doesn't matter at all if the *belief is true or not*.

If you believe something, it doesn't matter if you often hear otherwise - it has no impact on the subconscious. For example, suppose that you are absolutely convinced you are "useless and ugly." (This is actually a belief held by many people deep down in their soul. It is a widespread thought in depressive episodes.)

If you believe that, then it is absolutely, once and for all, *true* for you. It doesn't matter if reality confirms it or not. In fact, we tend to read situations in *that* way, which goes along with our *already formed* beliefs. Therefore, views strengthen over time if they are not challenged.

I love biographies. I love reading about people I admire. Some of these people are great artists, others famous faith leaders or politicians. Reading about them, I'm always amazed when I realize that their lives were *no piece of cake*. I know it's a bit stupid, but I tend to mostly assume that famous people don't have to deal with the difficulties I encounter. (In psychology, this is called a mastery-model. It's a common psychological bias.)

But that's absolutely not true. Quite the opposite, in fact.

If you read about famous people (in a real account and not some glossed-over piece of public relations), you see that they come across and sometimes stumble over the same conflicts you and I have. Especially in the arts, artists tend to see themselves as deficient - never good enough, never meeting their own expectations. That's the inner mantra many people have.

Actually, this is a kind of *self-abuse*. I remember listening to a great performance. Afterward, I went backstage to congratulate the performer. The artist said to me: "No, that was so bad — don't congratulate me. I'm sorry, I was such a mess." If this happens once, you might think it's just over the top humbleness. If it happens more often, you see that the other person *really believes* that.

And don't get fooled by a strong exterior either.

Many people in the public spotlight hide their insecurities behind a tough or even arrogant manner. On closer view, it's clear they are not nearly as confident as they seem. If you pay attention to news of this kind, you will realize how many people in the public eye suffer from depression, drug abuse, alcohol addiction, and so on. I think it's a powerful reminder that we all have to deal with similar difficult stuff in our lives.

Back to my affirmations.

Imagine you're absolutely convinced deep down that you're lazy, a lousy human being, and totally worthless. If someone tells you otherwise, trying to cheer you up, pointing out the positive aspects of yourself, your subconscious will powerfully interject: "You know that's false!"

Now imagine walking around your apartment and bumping into peppy messages all day. How would you feel? Which thoughts pop up in your mind?

It's excruciating! It's tormenting!

If your negative belief about yourself is strong, there will be a proper battle inside your psyche. Every positive affirmation will trigger a scream of "Not true!" by your subconscious. And this inner tug of war costs you lots of energy. It eats you inside out and results in massive inner tension.

In the end, your negative belief gets stronger because it fights tooth and nail for its survival. You get the opposite outcome from your well-intended positive affirmations. I know that's hard to hear because a whole industry of motivational speakers, self-help gurus, videos and pharmaceuticals, etc., builds on these (false) premises. It doesn't work that way. A study published in the journal *Psychological Science* confirmed it.[1]

So, the real questions are:

If positive affirmations don't work, what does? How do we get the strength to master stressful situations in the first place? How can we exceed our own expectations of ourselves? What inspires us to muster the energy to pull ourselves together and invest all we have in reaching for a goal? And why *should* we in the first place?

The short answer: It's a *process*.

(The long answer is this book.)

Humans are very complex creatures. There are libraries of philosophical works on the topic of human nature.[2] I don't feel comfortable telling you what human nature really is. Nevertheless, I do know that as humans, we can endure quite a lot of hardship if we see *some sort of sense* behind it.

American psychologist and therapist David Schnarch calls that "meaningful endurance."[3] Meaningful endurance is part of his theory of "four points of balance." In a nutshell, it means that we are able to face the music, step up and pull ourselves together - even if it is uncomfortable for us. But we do so only if we see the meaning behind it.

That in itself is quite remarkable.

You would think that our highest aim in life would be to live a life of leisure, not having to deal with any hardship. You would think that people are happiest when living in absolute comfort, being insulated from anything causing discomfort. You would think that a life without distress and worry should guarantee high spirits all year round.

Well, that's not true.

I'm a big fan of the movie "Matrix." (I know it's old, and I'm dating myself here.) Nevertheless, one of my favorite scenes is when the good guy Morpheus gets captured by bad Agent Smith.[4] Agent Smith then points to the matrix, this great illusion of reality, and tells him his philosophy on human nature:

Billions of people just living out their lives, oblivious. Did you know that the first Matrix was designed to be a perfect human world, where none suffered? Where everyone would be happy? It was a disaster. No one would accept the program. [...] I believe that, as a species, human beings define their reality through misery and suffering.

Of course, Agent Smith is the villain here, so don't take his words too seriously. In the movie, he is trying to break Morpheus' spirit at this point. But (in my opinion) villains frequently have the best lines in movies![5]

In fact, what he says is very thought-provoking. Agent Smith is right in the sense that suffering *defines* our existence. But contrary to his philosophy, that's actually a *good thing*. As humans, we have the ability to withstand hardship for the sake of internal development. We can face discomfort in order to grow.

In the long run, I think that's even the secret behind our adaptivity and success. We can adapt to an absolutely stunning range of circumstances and environments. All animals (and humans, too) try to avoid pain and maximize pleasure. This is why psychologists list "avoidance of pain" as one of the basic psychological needs for humans.[6]

More importantly, we can forego pleasure and choose to endure discomfort. Very often, there is something difficult or negative to go through to reach a goal. Nothing worthwhile in life comes easy. Our goals may have side effects to them, which are not entirely desirable. Psychologists call situations of this type approach-avoidance conflicts.[7]

We are not enslaved by a need for instant gratification. We can look hardship in the eye and brace ourselves for impact if we understand the necessity. I think that's essential for the pursuit of long-term goals. Furthermore, this is also the key to learning and teaching.

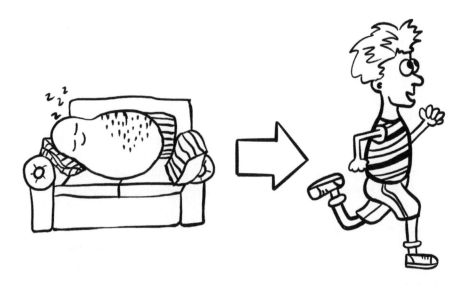

Couch potato or running?

If you want to learn something, you need *persistence*. In order to persist, you must see the *necessity* to do so. Teaching is assisted learning. As a teacher, you help a student to learn, nothing more. That's why motivation is so important. If your goals are in *alignment with the end result* of your learning, you will be motivated. You will be able to do what's needed to get there. As teachers, our job is to provide the necessary information and support for that.

The long-time goals we have are closely connected to the values we cherish. Values (like beliefs) are the basis of our identity. Quite often, our long-term goals conflict with short-term comfort. Why should I invest my time and energy into running if being a couch potato at home feels so much more comfortable? Why should I forego the instant feel-good factor of pizza in front of the TV? Why should I try to exercise and eat healthier?

You will only be able to motivate yourself to do so with *strong values*, such as if good health is important to you or a set of values exist in the background, which helps you override the initial discomfort.

Let's be honest, everything worthwhile in life requires dedication. If people tell you otherwise, they are lying. In order to achieve something, you have to commit. That's true for marriage, career, parenting, caring for others, learning a musical instrument, or generally developing your skills.

Discomfort, suffering, and hardship without a purpose are wasteful and foolish. Hardship in and of itself serves no meaning and accomplishes little to nothing. Don't waste your time on it.

Only if your values are strong enough will you be able to face hardship.

Most times, that's very demanding. I'm not trying to tell you it's a piece of cake. But it's much easier to accept discomfort if it's meaningful. It's easier if you can find consolation in the fact that what you do is in sync with your values. When there is a purpose, a long-term outcome you desire. When actually (in the end) something positive might be the result.

Important points to remember

✓ Our beliefs form a great deal of our identity. Beliefs are very resistant to change.

✓ As humans, we can endure quite a lot of hardship if we see some sort of sense behind it.

✓ If your goals align with the end result of your learning, you will be motivated.

✓ Discomfort and hardship without a purpose are wasteful and foolish.

Chapter references

1   The study can be found here: Senay, Ibrahim/Albarracín, Dolores/Noguchi Kenji: "Motivating Goal-Directed Behavior Through Introspective Self-Talk: The Role of the Interrogative Form of Simple Future Tense." In: Psychological Science, 21, 4, 499-504.

2   If you are interested, you can check out (as one example among many) the book "Man's Search for Meaning" by Viktor Frankl. Frankl writes about his experiences being a prisoner in Nazi concentration camps. He also lays out his psychotherapeutic method, which is based on finding purpose in life. He concludes that a sense of purpose directly impacted survival in a concentration camp. That may be a conclusion reaching too far: Also (as many critics have remarked), he has a bit of a habit of self-aggrandizement. Nevertheless, read with caution; it's an informative read.

3   The term "meaningful endurance" is part of Schnarch's theory of differentiation. I highly recommend his book: "Intimacy and desire."

4   Here is the link to this scene: https://www.youtube.com/watch?v=JrBdYmStZJ4.

5   As acting coach Ivana Chubbuck (2004) put it: "Even the most vicious criminals have a sympathetic reason for their behavior." It's this combination of good intention and doing evil, which I find very compelling.

6   You find this concept in Grawe's 2004 book on neuropsychotherapy.

7   The term was coined by Kurt Lewin in his ground-breaking 1935 book "A Dynamic Theory of Personality."

Chapter 4

Basic Needs and the 'Broccoli Vibe'

Learning is strongly connected to motivation: We need some kind of motivation to learn. This motivation can have many forms. Imagine you are suffering from arthritis - your joints hurt, they are stiff, and you can't take long walks. To reduce the pain, you decide to go to a special tai chi class for arthritis patients. Your pain gets better; you are happy.[1]

In this case, pain *reduction* is the motivation. But you can also be motivated by another gain, an *incentive*: Suppose you always wanted to learn how to paint. Finally, you decide to start and to go to a private class. Imagine your feeling when you finish your first painting!

Motivation is based on the individual's mental structure. It is also rooted in every single person's individual physical needs - every person is different. But overall, as humans, we try to avoid pain and gain pleasure. That's a common trait.

So, although we are all unique, there are some common traits among people. Dominance in traits changes over time - under varying circumstances, different personality traits pop to the front. During our personal development, we have distinct needs at different stages. A young kid requires different things than an adult.

That's actually quite a problem for teaching. Often, we realize the necessity to learn something relatively late. We look back and think, "Oh, I should have learned this years ago, I should have started when I was a kid (or when I was in school or ten years younger, etc.)."

Often, we realize only later what we could have accomplished if we had committed to something earlier. I've been thinking about this for a long time. It seems to me to be a crucial fact - our mental development lags behind. You can compare it to *chocolate*. Everybody loves chocolate, right? It's easy to get excited about sweets. They taste great, give you a sugar high, and are fun. It's much harder to get excited about — let's say — *broccoli* (dull, green, strange texture).

By the time you fully appreciate the virtue of eating broccoli, you might already have successfully conditioned yourself to eat lots of sweets. The same is true with learning. There are many things, which are designed to be like chocolate (exciting, fun, gives you a high) — such as online games. In comparison, many other useful activities have a distinct *broccoli vibe*.

At the period in our personal development when learning new things comes most easily (childhood), we are not interested in dull academic learning. Especially during our early childhood years, we are interested in many other things besides academics. The brain (being the wonderful instrument it is) dutifully absorbs everything it is exposed to as a sponge.

A group of researchers around Simone Kühn at the university clinic in Hamburg found that kids who "game" a lot have different brains.[2] We know that the only thing the brain cannot do is not learn. If you play *Super Mario* for hours, you will get a *Super Mario brain*. The structure of your brain reflects what you experience.

There are particular brain areas that are important for finger movement. I even heard that kids nowadays have high density in these areas. The brain areas concerned with thumb movement are noticeably thicker. They are thicker because people spent so many hours with their smartphones. They are virtuosos of *swipe right* and *swipe left*.

If I'm very motivated to 'game' and do so regularly, my brain will mirror this interest. If I'm motivated to learn tai chi, painting, or a foreign language, my brain will reflect this likewise. The problem I see is that not all these activities are equally *desirable*. In the case of smartphone games or social media, for example, these sites and games are psychologically designed to hook you. They want to maximize the time you spent there.

The longer you stay, the more you are exposed to add-time, etc. As long as you are on their site, you are generating revenue for these companies. They use a *lot* of motivation psychology to keep you there. It's a business model — and it has a great impact. At the moment, many people discuss whether social media is addictive. Which impact does it have on mental health and self-esteem? What can we do about it?[3]

For teachers, this is a big problem because we want to be good and effective teachers. We know the importance of motivation, and we try our best. But we also know that we compete against many other activities. Many of these activities are products, which are tailor-made to suit the basic needs of the people using them. They use *instant gratification* to keep users on their platforms.

As a teacher, it is tough to compete with that, which can be frustrating. You might feel like you offer something of immense value, but unfortunately, your "product" feels outdated, under-marketed, and dull in comparison to all the shiny, gratifying virtual realms.

Still, I'm optimistic.

Since motivation is key to learning, we must figure out what makes the learners (as persons) tick. We must try to understand their motivation. Only then are we able to effectively help them. This seems obvious but is rather hard in reality.

Where should we start? How can we figure out what motivates people? An excellent way to understand other people's motivations is to look for basic needs. Basic needs are crucial - everyone has basic needs. We must analyze what they are and if they are met. Then we have a chance to understand (on a very elementary level) how people are motivated.

'Elementary level' is not meant disparagingly here. As human beings, we have basic needs. There's a bit of a discussion on what may count as a basic need. Obviously, we need food, shelter, etc. If you are hungry and have no place to live, it's a miserable existence. If you have no chance to rest or are too cold, you will die. These are basic needs at the core - they are *existential*.

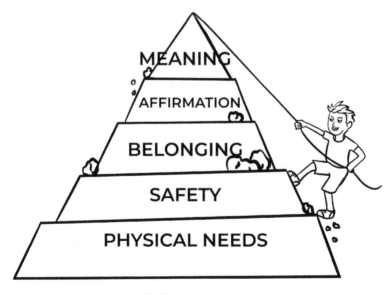

Climbing Mt. Maslow.

The concept of basic needs is most famously connected to Abraham Maslow. [4] He postulated a hierarchy of needs, a pyramid. In this pyramid, one layer of needs has to be met in order to proceed to the next level. Maslow started at the bottom of his pyramid with what he called "physiological" needs (food, water, warmth, rest). Located on the next layer, are "safety" needs, meaning our need to be free of immediate danger. We need to feel secure - it's no fun to live in constant anxiety.

If our safety needs are met, Maslow says, we try to fulfill social needs. Social needs include a broad spectrum. In Maslow's context, it means we need to have meaningful intimate relationships. He called that "belonging and love". Or as the kids sing: "Sitting in the tree, K-i-s-s-i-n-g!".

Besides social needs, we also try to boost our self-esteem. We want to accomplish something; we strive for prestige and social recognition. There is an internal drive, which makes us try to impress people. For humans, social status is very important. This may be an ancient heritage from our ancestors. Evolutionarily, it is very important for a single individual to know its place on the social ladder.

Our brain is a *social brain* formed through social interactions with other people, our parents, friends, etc. It is geared to ensure our survival through social behavior. There are special brain areas, which process social information. Some brain regions are specialized to "read" faces, to guess what other people think and feel. The rank of individuals on the social ladder is assessed in the reward system. [5]

So, our social rank, how people react to us and how others see us, is very important to us - the higher up on the ladder, the better. This makes sense. In ancient times, living in rather small tribal groups, we might have had better survival chances as high-ranking members of our group. If we are honest, it's not much different today. The higher up you are, the stronger your claim on scarce resources is.

Most people try to boost their social standing by pursuing their professional careers. Often the level of their self-esteem is connected to professional success. On a bigger scale, society as a whole is the same. I always found it very revealing that we ask, "What is he or she *worth*?" Success and perception of worthiness are strongly connected in our culture.

When we have accomplished what we wanted to pursue and when we have worked on our self-esteem, we reach the tip of Maslow's pyramid. There at the tip, Maslow saw his theory of "self-actualization." Self-actualization is a grand term. It means the fulfillment of our full potential, the realization of our creativity in all its forms. In Maslow's theory, it's like the prize you get after going through all the other levels.

This pyramid is a very neat idea. It has many merits.

What I very much like about it is that it allows us to think about our needs in the first place! If you think about it. In our society, our needs are normally of little concern overall. Most of the time, we know exactly what we *have* to do, what we *should* do, and what we are *expected* to do. What we really *want* to do is sometimes not so easy to know.

So, I think it was a significant step forward to put needs on the table as a topic.

The problem I have is the neat pyramid. Some scientists jokingly call it "climbing Mt. Maslow." But life is not like that. Life is not ascension towards a summit. Life is not as clean as in an online game, where you gain skills, survive a boss fight, and then proceed to the next level. To be fair, Maslow's theory has changed over the years, and it was (and still is) very influential.

I find Maslow's model especially interesting when applied to relationships. Nowadays, relationships with other people are often entered to fulfill esteem and self-actualization needs:[6] We want to be friends with people who reflect our best selves. We want to study with famous teachers. We want to marry a person who elevates us.

These higher-level needs of self-esteem and self-actualization typically involve a rather substantial mutual investment of energy and time. If this investment is made, deep attachment and insight into the other person's qualities can be the reward. The categories (in the way Maslow proposed) are most likely correct. I think that they can also overlap. They are not a neat pyramid shape. Rather, you can switch back and forth between levels.

It is entirely possible to go back from an "upper" level to a "lower" level. Imagine, for example, that you fear losing your job. Your boss sends you an email asking you to come by the office. In your brain, you go through all your last interactions; you analyze and wreck your brain searching for hints and clues — "what could have happened? What could be the case?" You think about your company - maybe sales are bad. Perhaps there is tough competition. There are many things to think about.

One moment, you were on the tip of Maslow's pyramid, happily working on your self-actualization. The next moment (after the email), you are forced to grapple with basic needs for safety and security (while you still have your job!). It's clear that our needs are not as static as they may seem. There is a lot of fluctuation in them. Our needs change according to the circumstances we find ourselves in.[7]

Apart from the way Maslow sees our needs in the rather static terms of a pyramid, I was bothered for a long time by the "ultimate goal" of self-actualization. It seemed so selfish to me that our main purpose should be simply to fulfill ourselves! It never really met my own outlook towards life. Of course, "self-actualization" is a broad term; it can mean a lot of things. But I think there must be more to life. Maybe you can self-actualize by doing something meaningful, contributing to society, getting involved?

Then recently, I stumbled upon a passage in a book. This passage said the same thing! (Imagine my joy, what a boost to *my* self-esteem.) This passage did not only argue similarly to what I felt was right, but it also seems that Maslow himself (as he got older) rethought his claims concerning self-actualization.[8]

According to his later writings, we find our fullest realization in being part of something greater than ourselves. You can call that transcendence, spirituality, or altruism - the name doesn't matter. I very much like that idea. And I find it telling that Maslow himself revised his theory. Maybe it is just romantic thinking, but perhaps Maslow saw that people had misunderstood his writings. He felt the need to clarify that the self-actualization he meant is actually something bigger.

I'm absolutely convinced that this is true. I'm sure that giving and sharing are core points of our being as humans. The joy you feel in giving a gift to someone is wonderful. Maybe it's even better than getting a gift yourself.

I'm asking you, why else become a teacher?

Becoming a teacher takes a long time.

It pays badly.

And is stressful.

But it gives us a unique privilege. As teachers, we can catch a glimpse of the future. We see the next generation of students. We can offer them guidance, try to nurture them, offer them perspectives they hadn't previously seen. We can do our best to make a difference. We can invest in the common good by trying to lift up the learners.

I'm 100% convinced that teachers should be paid better. I'm absolutely sure teachers should have less stress. I also think that teaching is great. If working on our mutual future doesn't count as transcendence, I don't know what does.

Maslow and his theory are the topics of much discussion in the academic field. There is also a lot of criticism, I admit. What I find interesting, though, is that Maslow is also very influential outside the academic bubble. It seems like he struck a chord.

Many people not connected to the ivory tower refer to his ideas frequently. His name pops up in political arguments, management discussions, and so forth. That alone shows his significance. Maslow changed the way we think about basic needs.

Important points to remember

✓   We need some kind of motivation in order to learn. Motivation can have many forms.

✓   According to Maslow, we have basic needs: Physiological and safety needs, love and belongingness, self-esteem, reputation and self-actualization.

✓   Our brain is a social brain.

✓   We find our fullest realization in being part of something greater than ourselves.

Chapter references

1   If you wonder — it really helps! Here is a study on the matter: Wang C, Schmid CH, Iversen MD, Harvey WF, Fielding RA, Driban JB, Price LL, Wong JB, Reid KF, Rones R, McAlindon T. (2016): "Comparative effectiveness of Tai Chi versus physical therapy for knee osteoarthritis: a randomized trial." *Ann Intern Med*; 165:77-86.

2   You can find the study here: Kühn, S., Gleich, T., Lorenz, R. C., Lindenberger, U., & Gallinat, J. (2014): "Playing Super Mario induces structural brain plasticity: Gray matter changes resulting from training with a commercial video game." *Molecular Psychiatry*, 19, 265-271. doi:10.1038/mp.2013.120

3   Here is an interesting study on this subject: Hou, Youbo & Xiong, Dan & Jiang, Tonglin & Song, Lili & Wang, Qi. (2019): "Social media addiction: Its impact, mediation, and intervention". *Cyberpsychology: Journal of Psychosocial Research on Cyberspace*. 13. 10.5817/CP2019-1-4

4   See Maslow, A (1954): *Motivation and personality*. New York, NY: Harpe

5   This is an excellent article on this topic: Munuera, J., Rigotti, M. & Salzman, C.D. (2018): "Shared neural coding for social hierarchy and reward value in primate amygdala." *Nat Neurosci* 21, 415–423 (2018). https://doi.org/10.1038/s41593-018-0082-8

6   A very insightful article on Maslow and the implications of his theory on long-term relationships can be found here: Finkel, E., Hui, C.M., Carswell, K.L., & Larson, G.M. (2014): "The Suffocation of Marriage: Climbing Mount Maslow Without Enough Oxygen." *Psychological Inquiry*, 25, 1 - 41.

7   Recently, Kaufman made a 21st-century update to Maslow. It is a very interesting read: Kaufman, Scott Barry (2020): *Transcend. The New Science of Self-Actualization*. New York, NY: TarcherPerigee.

8   You find the quote here: Maslow, Abraham H. (1996). "Critique of self-actualization theory". In E. Hoffman (ed.). *Future visions: The unpublished papers of Abraham Maslow*. Thousand Oaks, CA: Sage. pp. 26–32.

Chapter 5
It's Not All About Broccoli:
Basic Psychological Needs

Basic needs are very important. They are a good tool to try to make sense of other people's behavior and our own too! When you ask yourself, "Which needs do I have? Which needs are active right now?" you get a better understanding for yourself. You can see more clearly, what influences how you behave and which deeper layers of your soul are involved.

The same is true for learners. We are all constantly learning. We are all learners if we like it or not. We have basic needs. Our students also have basic needs. It seems like my needs as a teacher and the students' needs rule each other out more often than not. (I don't think that's necessarily the case. The crucial point is to strike a good balance between these different poles — more on that later.)

Let's look deeper into basic psychological needs and what they mean for teaching.

Maslow was a big step forward, bringing basic needs to everyone's attention. In my opinion, if you dig a little deeper and focus on the *psychological needs*, it gets even more interesting. All our needs are somehow reflected in our psyche.

We have senses - we see, feel, and taste our world. Through our senses, the brain receives input from the outside. Based on this input (and with a lot of data scrubbing), the mind builds an internal representation of our world. Our experiences, our dreams, and our aspirations are all incorporated into this representation.

Today, psychologists think that we have four basic human psychological needs:[1]

- Control/orientation
- Pleasure/avoidance of pain
- Self-enhancement
- Attachment

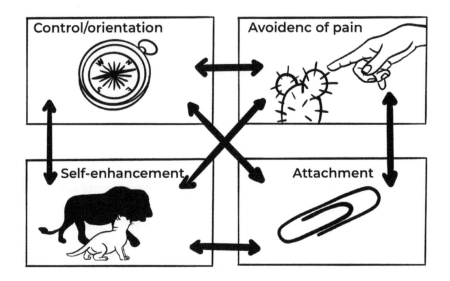

Basic psychological needs.

Looking closely, you see there is a lot of Maslow in this list. "Control and orientation" resembles Maslow's "safety and security." The point here is that it is meant mentally. With control and orientation, you *feel* a certain degree of control over your surroundings. You feel somewhat in charge. You can influence your environment to make it better suit your needs.

Suppose you are going on a roller coaster - a thrilling experience! By getting on this thing, you have the thrill of stepping out of your usual comfort zone. It's fun, it's exciting. But, you must accept helplessness. You are tied to a seat and will be flung at top speed with Gs.

That accounts for the adrenaline kick. But now, control and orientation come into play. You would never use a roller coaster not tested by authorities, right? You might go bungee jumping, but you would, of course, use a proper cord. (And not something you got at your local arts and crafts.) So, part of the thrill is that you know deep down that (emergencies aside) nothing *really* serious can happen to you.

That's the reason why bungee jumping is not traumatic for you (if you like this type of thing — I'm afraid of heights, so I don't count). It's not traumatic because the danger is contained. Actually, we experience *simulated danger*. That's why bungee jumping is fun and walking at night in a bad part of town is not. In our personal fantasy, the danger at night is very much *real*.

If you think back to the roller coaster, you get on it, and at any given moment, you are sure that you can pull the emergency brake. You can call assistance and even get a refund (if something was amiss). So you have the thrill, but the probability of something bad happening is actually rather slim.

I think that's also the nice thing about horror movies. You might get scared a bit, but the only thing really threatening you is overdosing on popcorn and coke. For our distant ancestors, dangers were far more real and heftier than for us. For them, being gobbled up by a lion or a bear might have been a real danger. For us, it's not. The dangers we are in are existential (if you think about climate change, maybe even more so). At the same time, these dangers are more abstract.

The important argument is that we need to feel we are *somewhat in control*. We need to know where we are (orientation). Disorientation is actually a severe symptom in several psychological diseases. If we don't feel in control, we are helpless. And that's very harmful to our soul.

A strong part of the trauma experience is the feeling of helplessness, of being overpowered by someone. Incidents like this can leave deep scars in a person's psyche. No matter what you try to do, you cannot alleviate your situation.

That's a powerful feeling.

As humans, we try our best to avoid situations like that. We work hard not to get into a position of helplessness. I'm sure that's the deeper reason for many of the things we try to achieve (wealth, power, a good career). We try to achieve them because subconsciously, we try to keep ourselves from being helpless.

Deep down, we know that if you have money, you have the financial means to cope with difficult situations. If you are poor and lose your job, it's an existential threat to you. If you are rich and lose your job, it's less life-threatening. At least, that's the way we often think. (In reality, rich people have a lot of other problems.)

Still, helplessness is an intense stressor. We try to avoid it because we don't like to feel pain. From the perspective of evolution, pain is a very useful sensation. It shows us that we are doing something wrong. If we eat too many sweets, we feel sick. Our body tells us that it was too much. We don't like that feeling, so (maybe) we don't do it again.

So, we arrive at the second basic psychological need: "Pleasure and avoidance of pain."

People like pleasure:[2] It's so basic to our existence that we rarely ask ourselves why this is the case. We like pleasure, and we are not the only ones! Other animals with consciousness also seek pleasurable experiences. Most likely, pleasure is a system of positive feedback. It feels good, and this positive feeling motivates us to do it again, to revisit an enjoyable situation.

We try to recreate circumstances that we have found to be positive and worth seeking. We like situations, which make us happy. We want to be entertained. We like to get our kicks (whatever works for you individually).

On the flip side, we do our best to avoid pain.

We don't like to suffer, and we are willing to go to great lengths to dodge painful situations. At least, normally, we do our best to avoid threatening circumstances. In reality, though, it's quite complicated. Seldom is a situation that simple. We must be willing to accept a certain amount of pain to get the desired result. Think about the workplace. Talking to your boss might be painful, but it cannot be avoided if you want a raise.

There is a whole theory based on this effect, called the *somatic marker hypothesis*.[3] Somatic means bodily. The idea is that we sense at any given moment how we are *through our bodies*. The way we feel inside our bodies serves as a reference to judge a situation.

Think about it - if you are anxious, your legs are wobbly, and your stomach feels weird. If you are in love, you get butterflies in your stomach. If you are depressed, you feel like the weight of the whole world rests on your shoulders. It's really easy to find lots of examples. These feelings are markers; they mark a situation as pleasurable or unpleasurable.

All these situations are connected to body sensations. We can describe the situations through the body sensations they are connected to. The way we feel marks the situation and places a label on it. And the markers help us to *decide* if we want to experience a situation again or not.

If we feel happy, excited, or euphoric, we most likely will try to go there again. That's why (if you *like* roller coasters), you finish one round and think, "Let's do that once more, immediately!" (in science, this phenomenon is called *approach behavior*).

On the other side, if something has been a painful, negative experience for us, we will certainly try to avoid it. We will avoid doing that again. If you *don't like* roller coasters, but were peer-pressured into one, barely keeping hold of your lunch — well, you finish that round and think, "Never, ever will I do *that* again!"

As you can see, pleasure is highly subjective. The same things can be pleasurable for one person and uncomfortable for another.

Pleasure is key to our emotional lives. We have a whole system in our brains, which is almost exclusively occupied with it - the reward system. The reward system is a group of brain structures, which make us feel pleasure.

Therefore, the reward system is very important for motivation and learning. If a situation gives us pleasure, we will want to revisit it. Physiologically this means that inside the brain, a very complex process has taken place. The situation was assessed, and the reward system has released neurotransmitters, which make us feel good.

To make matters even more complicated, pleasure is not always connected to things happening to us from the outside. We can feel very pleased about something we have accomplished, a situation we handled well, or a good idea we had. And if you remember Maslow, we have the need to self-actualize, fulfill our destiny, or find our calling.

This is because of the third basic psychological need: the need for "self-enhancement."

Self-enhancement is again a grand term (like self-actualization). It means quite simply that we want to *feel good about ourselves*. We have several identities within ourselves - we have a private self, a professional self, a self as a family member, a friend, a partner, and so forth. Within these identities, we strive to be in sync with our values.

Identity and values come from our upbringing - we are influenced by our family, the schools we attended, and our friends. Some of it we may get genetically handed down from earlier generations and some we may get from our friends. Then we have the influential movies we watch, books we read, and people we meet. Throw in all the other experiences we make throughout our lives, and our identity is a huge pot.

The important idea is that we like to be good people. If you look at popular culture, you see that cartoon villains are often very boring. They are not exciting if they are simply bad guys. They are thrilling, electrifying characters if they have a story, a history behind them. You wonder, "Why are they bad? Where did they turn to the wrong side? What would I do in their shoes?"

In my opinion, the most interesting villains are the ones, which are totally convinced that what they do is actually *good*.[4] Within their own framework of thinking, they are the good guys. They believe without a shred of doubt that what they do is positive. So by doing the evilest things, they are sure they are pushing a positive agenda.

It is us, seeing them from the outside, who understand the evil in their doing.

Apart from comic book villains, you will see that also in real life. People who do atrocious things often have some kind of backstory, which (in their minds) justifies their deeds. As humans, they need that. They need to feel optimistic about what they do. It is important to their self-esteem.

The same with us. We want to boost our self-esteem with something positive, doing meaningful work, contributing to society (that's Maslow's transcendence). Sometimes, people with a more cynical worldview find that ridiculous. They argue that in the end, it's all meaningless anyway.

I disagree. Interestingly, it seems like we have the need to contribute and help others deeply embedded within ourselves. A lot of research is done in this field, the study of altruism. Altruism means that we are concerned about the well-being and happiness of others. For example, it looks like kids are in and of themselves "altruistic."[5]

Now, don't get me wrong, if you have kids, I'm sure you will agree. Kids can be the most selfish people on the whole planet! (At least, it may seem so). On the other hand, there is reliable research that shows young kids are very social. Kids as young as one and a half years old help others in need.[6] They do that without any apparent gain for themselves and without a reward offered. It may even be the case that the offer of a reward *undermines* the helping behavior!

Of course, it's impossible to know for sure what's going on in their minds. These kids are so young; they can't even talk! But it seems they are not expecting any form of return on their investment. They are not concerned with their reputation or getting into anyone's good books. They simply do it. It seems to be a natural tendency.

It's really remarkable that chimpanzees, our nearest relatives in the animal kingdom, also do that. They similarly help each other, for example by using tools. (Another thing they have in common with us is that they are capable of absolutely atrocious behavior.)

As kids grow older, these naturally altruistic tendencies wear off. Researchers think this may be due to socialization and social feedback. We are inherently altruistic, but then we unlearn it. We experience situations and behaviors, which make us lose our tendency towards altruism. I find that stunning.

We must be cautious not to romanticize childhood. We should not see kids as somehow better human beings. Rather, I would suggest that we think very hard about the kind of experiences we make on our path to adulthood. What do we experience, and which situations form our values and our identity?

We become who we are not through ourselves alone - we inherit the genes from our family. Besides and on top of that, we form our identity and our values by living with others. Humans are social animals.[7] We are socialized and embedded into the culture of the group we are born into.

Later in our individual development, we can reflect and criticize this culture. But at first, we are utterly dependent on the support and the good-will of the people around us. So, the altruism we show as infants may not truly be selfless - it might rather be a very good evolutionary strategy to survive.

When babies are born, they are helpless. Humans (opposed to other species) are born too early. As anthropologist Adolf Portmann pointed out, we are biologically defined by our shortcomings.[8] We need a reliable support system in order to survive infancy. We must form strong relationships with others very early in our development.

This leads to the last basic psychological need: "Attachment."
Among the basic psychological needs, *attachment* is the need best studied and most proven scientifically. Already more than 60 years ago, John Bowlby and Mary Ainsworth started research on this topic. They worked with children who had lost their parents during the Second World War.

These kids were well cared for *physically*. They were orphans, but great efforts were undertaken to provide them with the necessities of life. The question for Bowlby and Ainsworth was. How would they fare *psychologically* in later life? Having lost their parents, how would their path through life be?

These orphans had gone through severe trauma — they had lost their parents after all. Bowlby and Ainsworth asked, Who of these orphans could proceed to live a relatively "normal" life? And who wasn't? And especially, for which reason?

As a result of their studies, Bowlby and Ainsworth formulated *attachment theory*. They were sure that the experiences we make early in our lives form our outlook on life. We continually assess what is happening to us. Very early, this constitutes *a way of assessment, a style,* how we see others and their behavior towards us.

Especially important are the closest caregivers in our early lives - we attach ourselves to them. We bond. These attachment figures can be the biological parents, but not necessarily so. The definition of attachment is simply *our capacity to form a bond with other people.* We can link with others, and we do that specifically when we are very small.

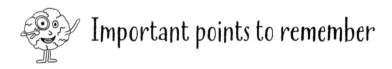# Important points to remember

✓   We have four basic human psychological needs:
- Control/orientation
- Pleasure/avoidance of pain
- Self-enhancement
- Attachment

✓   A vital part of trauma is the feeling of helplessness, of being overpowered by someone.

✓   Emotions are somatic markers. The somatic marker hypothesis says that the way we feel inside our bodies serves as a reference to judge a situation. If it's pleasurable, we seek it. If it's painful, we avoid it.

✓   Pleasure is key to our emotional lives. The reward system in our brains is almost exclusively occupied with it.

✓   Humans are social animals. We form beliefs (about us and others) through social interaction.

✓   We need a reliable support system in order to survive infancy. We must form strong relationships with others very early in our development.

Chapter references

1   See Grawe (2004, 186) for reference,

2   A good book on this topic is Linden, David J. (2011): *Pleasure: how our brains make junk food, exercise, marijuana, generosity, and gambling feel so good*. Richmond: Oneworld.

3   It was first formulated by Antonio Damasio and his team in 1991. As with everything in science, there is some discussion about it. You can watch Damasio's TED-Talk if you like. Or read his book from 1994/2008: Descartes' Error: Emotion, Reason and the Human Brain.

4   The Joker from Batman comes to my mind.

5   A seminal paper in this regard is Warneken, F. and Tomasello, M. (2009), The roots of human altruism. British Journal of Psychology, 100: 455-471. doi:10.1348/000712608X379061

6   You can check out the video here: https://www.youtube.com/watch?v=Z-eU5xZW7cU

7   This idea goes (at least) as far back as Aristotle, who saw human beings as political and social animals: Zoon politikon (ζῷον πολιτικόν).

8   Portmann explains his ideas in his classic book: Portmann, Adolf (1956): *Zoologie und das neue Bild des Menschen*. Biologische Fragmente zu einer Lehre vom Menschen. Frankfurt: Rowohlt.

Chapter 6
The Lifeblood of Relationships: Attachment

Attachment is our capacity to form a bond with other people. It's the link connecting us to others. These links can last a lifetime and can connect us over long distances and long periods of time. Once we have formed an attachment, the bond can remain even when the attachment figure has already passed away. This is because attachment is a *psychological* phenomenon, not a *biological* one.

The natural purpose of attachment seems to be to keep kids close to their caregivers. For our early ancestors, this would boost the chances of their survival in hostile surroundings. In an evolutionary sense, the survival of our kids keeps our genes in the gene pool.

Bowlby believed that we have a drive to bond with important people around us - we have this drive from birth. Today, scientists think that these bonds start even earlier. There is good evidence that attachment already begins to form in the mother's womb:[1] Attachment is a fact of life.

The core idea of attachment theory states that if primary caregivers are there and attune to the kids' needs, they develop a sense of security; in attachment theory lingo, that's called "*responsivity*." If we as adults respond to our kids, and they honestly feel that we are reliable partners, they can grow to their full potential.

The experiences we have form our expectations. Prior experiences are the basis on which we judge new situations. If our long-term experience proves that we are respected and that people care for us, we will accordingly form a (positive) self-image.

If we make experiences over a longer period of time, we will form an according self-image.

Conversely, if we are poorly treated for long enough, we will likely incorporate this into our belief-system. We will think that we are not worthy of respect or that we are lacking something.

The present is the past of the future. I always try to keep in mind that the experiences students make with me now will impact how they assess themselves (and situations they will find themselves in) in the future. I have the chance to have some impact on their belief-systems by being mindful and responsive.

Think about responsivity as a response in dialogue. It does not mean that we parrot what the other person says; it means that we earnestly and honestly try to answer. This allows others to establish a *secure basis* to operate from. Studies have shown caregivers' level of responsivity is a valid indicator for secure attachment in kids.

Please don't get me wrong - responsivity is not catering to all the whims of your child. Actually, if you do that, you might even *harm* your child in the long run. Attachment theory says that we have to be responsive. Responding can mean a lot of things in different circumstances.

Quite often, people ask me for patent remedies. They don't exist. There is no sure formula, and there are no hard and fast rules. Every situation is different; every kid is different, and every adult is different. What has worked on one day can fail later on.

On one day, being responsive may mean giving in to your child. On another, to draw a red line. Unfortunately, we must go through this inner insecurity. No one can really stop us from doubting whether we are doing the right thing or not.

On the positive side, if you're striving to work towards secure attachment, the (scientific) odds are with you.

Attachment is nowadays the best-documented and most systematically researched basic human need. Attachment theory finds more and more use in clinical practice, not only for kids but also for adults and seniors. The attachment quality of care seems to be a critical factor for human development. It's not only important for kids; we see its relevance from pre-birth to elderly care.

As a teacher, attachment theory was a revelation to me - it just makes so much sense! I had often wondered why some students could withstand serious levels of stress — and others can't. I had often wondered why some students have a more positive outlook towards their future than others. I had often wondered why some students achieve more academic success.

Today, I'm pretty convinced this has to do with their attachment styles. If you've had a positive experience that others are there for you, this belief stays with you your whole life. If you've had an experience that you can influence situations significantly, this belief also stays with you. If you've experienced the feeling that you are a worthy human being, this belief will remain with you as well.

Attachment is obviously significant. The other three basic psychological needs (control/orientation, pleasure/avoidance of pain, self-enhancement) are equally vital - there is no ladder or hierarchy among them. All four are essential. One of them may be dominant at a given time, but overall all are essential.

For example, if you feel as if you're in *danger*, your need for control and orientation will be heightened. If you feel *disrespected* at your workplace, your need for self-enhancement will be strong. If you feel *hurt* physically or psychologically, you will try to avoid similar situations. If you suffer from a *break-up*, your attachment needs will be prominent.

If you look closely at any given situation, you will see that (in absolutely most cases) *all* the basic psychological needs are somehow involved. Here a positive example: Imagine you have a lesson with a great teacher. The teacher makes you feel accepted; you like going there, and you have the feeling, "Here, I'm really being helped." Most likely, you will develop a secure attachment towards this teacher.

Since you like seeing this teacher and feel that you're accepted the way you are, your basic need for control and orientation is also fulfilled. At any given moment, you know that you can say if something is disturbing to you. If the secure attachment is provided, the situation feels already much more controlled - you are oriented. You know where you stand.

If you feel securely attached and in control/oriented, you can cope with criticism much better. As I said, teaching is assisted learning. My job as a teacher is to engineer a learning climate, which allows the learners to grow. Avoidance of pain and seeking pleasure is a very important psychological tool for that. Quite often, it is simply a manner of how I phrase criticism - I would suggest praising rather than criticizing. Criticism should always be worded with care. It should be given with the intention to help. It should never put additional obstacles in front of the student.[2]

Mostly, performance is a mixed bag. There are good aspects, and there are bad aspects. When students perform for me, I must (sometimes very quickly!) make up my mind what to say. Students are waiting for a response, a validation, an acknowledgment. I can choose to try to use negative reinforcement. In this case, I will reduce negative behavior by giving critique. Most likely, the student will try to change my critique's point (to avoid further scolding).

If I use positive reinforcement (praise), I use the opposite approach - I praise the positive aspects, hoping to strengthen these parts of the performance. The student will most likely try to show more of those behaviors, which have led to being praised. The student will be more motivated and will learn easier. *A happy brain likes to learn.*

Keeping the third basic psychological need in mind ("need for self-enhancement"), that makes absolute sense - we want to feel good about ourselves. We want to feel like we can achieve something. We want to see and feel that we *matter*. Getting positive feedback is crucial for that. As teachers, we must consciously build the students' self-esteem. Good self-esteem boosts our capability to accept valid critique.

If you consider a negative situation, you will also see that all the basic psychological needs are involved. Imagine your boyfriend or girlfriend is breaking up with you. You lose a close relationship in your life, and your attachment needs are hurt.

When someone breaks up with you, you are in a position of powerlessness. The other person is breaking up with you, and (in most cases) there is precious little you can do about it. You have no control over the situation. In desperation, you might try to win your former partner back in an attempt to reestablish control.

A break-up is also a very harmful experience - it hurts a lot. Sometimes people are hurt so much and so often that they decide to be done with relationships altogether. Hearing that always breaks my heart. To avoid further pain, they would rather quit the whole circus.

Lastly, a break-up is a giant blow to self-esteem. Often, questions are pondered neverendingly, "What happened?", "What went wrong with us?", "what did I do wrong?" After such a crucial life event (depending on the relationship's seriousness), the whole personality structure can be in shambles.

So mostly, all four basic psychological needs are involved in most significant situations. Even if one basic psychological need may dominate at one point, all four are equal - they are fundamental. The personality may collapse if under too much strain. There are very severe consequences if even one of these needs is not fulfilled for a longer period of time.

Important points to remember

✓   Attachment is our capacity to form a bond with other people. It's the link connecting us to others. These links can last a lifetime.

✓   If primary caregivers are responsive to childrens' needs, then children develop a sense of security. "Responsivity" fosters secure attachment.

✓   Attachment is nowadays the best-documented and most systematically researched basic human need.

✓   Attachment is obviously very important. The other three basic psychological needs (control/orientation, pleasure/avoidance of pain, self-enhancement) are equally vital.

✓   The whole personality structure can dissolve if basic psychological needs are not met for a longer period of time.

Chapter references

1 For more information, see Cataudella, Stefania & Lampis, Jessica & Busonera, Alessandra & L., Marino & Zavattini, Giulio Cesare. (2016): "From parental-fetal attachment to a parent-infant relationship: A systematic review about prenatal protective and risk factors." *Life Span and Disability*. XIX. 185-219.

2 See Butzkamm, Wolfgang (2012): *Lust zum Lehren, Lust zum Lernen: Eine neue Methodik für den Fremdsprachenunterricht*. Tübingen: Francke.

Chapter 7
What Makes Us Who We Are?
— Personal Growth

The basic psychological needs (attachment, control/orientation, avoidance of pain, self-enhancement) are the building blocks of our well-being. The whole personality structure may crumble if these needs are not met long-term.

That's looking at it negatively.

On the positive side, these basic psychological needs offer tremendous opportunities for personal growth. Researchers Grossmann & Grossmann have studied attachment for decades. They conclude that positive, secure relationships have a strong impact on success in learning.[1]

If you look at the studies they cite, it is clear that attachment and learning need to go *hand in hand*. Kids learn a lot of things like that, just by trying out how something works - in science, this is called exploration. If students have a secure attachment, they are more able to explore. Exploration in itself is learning. Maybe exploration is even the best way of learning. When we explore, we learn according to our own needs, at our own speed and in our own direction.

Learning is the basis of our existence. We need the ability to learn in order to grow, to be able to accomplish things and to understand. Learning itself is neutral - the brain doesn't distinguish if something is good for us or bad. It simply files away experiences. If experiences have been important to us, they are stored in the brain.

Learning can occur because we want to learn something — it's called *intentional learning*. Imagine you're planning a vacation in France and you would like to be able to say at least a few French words. You download a learning app on your phone.

You study dutifully, earning badges and points, getting more and more comfortable with the foreign language. You consciously commit vocabulary to your brain.

In this case, you've learned intentionally as preparation for your trip. Hopefully, you will be able to stun everyone in France with your language skills! But learning can also be just by accident, casually. We didn't *mean* to learn something, but we *did*.

Imagine you join a sports club; let's say, boxing. Of course, by joining a boxing club, training there, being coached, and you learn a lot about the sport of your choice. You also learn about social interactions, the etiquette of your sport, rules, hierarchy, etc.

In comparison, if you join a tennis or golf club, you will meet different people there. Different social rules apply; you must behave differently to fit in. You will learn that immediately (if you want to stay). This is called *informal* or *incidental learning*.

The third way of learning is implicit learning. Implicit means that we learn something without consciously meaning to. In a joyful, game-like manner, kids do that all the time. Believe me, as a parent (and I'm sure all the other parents out there agree), this can sometimes lead you to the brink of a nervous breakdown.

Kids have this absolutely astonishing capability - they can find surprising new uses for a whole lot of things. Most of the time (it seems), they intentionally search for ways, which maximize the effort needed to clean up afterward. Sometimes, simply moving the house seems like less of an effort!

The point is that we can casually learn a lot. Often, I find that learning casually is the most underrated way of learning! It is very useful and doesn't feel like a terrible burden. As I said, a happy brain likes to learn; if you do something you like, you will learn without any apparent effort.

Let's look again at the example of learning a foreign language. By all means, you need to learn vocabulary (if people tell you otherwise, they are lying). However, you can learn *a lot* about a foreign language by watching sit-coms, movies, or listening to others speak. It's a kind of low-key, low-threshold learning, which is enormously effective.

On the most basic level, learning is the connection of nerve cells (plasticity). Our brain has a lot of nerve cells! Scientists have counted them - there are 86 billion neurons in the human brain.[2]

This number is stunning. A billion is a thousand millions. I always have problems envisioning the difference. Think of it in terms of time - a *million* seconds is roughly 11 and a half days. A *billion* seconds is about 32 years. So 86 billion nerve cells in the brain is truly a lot.

This number is even more remarkable if you compare it to the actual size of our brains. Make your hands into fists, put them together at the knuckles (in front of your body) and look at them. Your brain inside the skull is not much bigger than that! Isn't it amazing?

The basic structures and connections inside the brain are more or less a given when we are born. How our brains *develop* depends highly on which kind of surroundings we have as kids. How functional our brains get is due to input. If we grow up in an environment rich in exciting stuff to explore, our brains will form connections accordingly.

If we grow up in an environment, which has little to excite us (an "impoverished environment"), our brains will be much less interconnected - nerve cells react to stimulation. If something happens a few times in a row, neurons will form new pathways. If something is very interesting, neurons will form new pathways. And if something is emotionally charged, neurons will form new pathways.

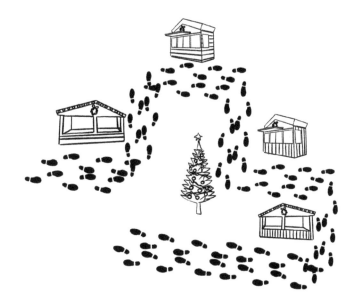

New neural pathways are like a snowy Christmas market: Paths often walked are imprinted more strongly.

These new neural pathways are like a snowy Christmas market.[3] Imagine the footprints in the snow left by customers. People are strolling around, leaving footprints, walking from hut to hut. At the end of the day, the Christmas market square is full of tracks.

You can see which huts are the most interesting for people - the tracks leading to the most interesting or frequented huts are *strong*. The trails leading to less popular huts are *weak*. You can see which paths are the most trodden - where many people went; there are many footprints.

The brain works similarly.

If a path is often walked upon, there will be many footprints. The footprints are like the new brain connections. Experiences we frequently make (walking in the snowy square) result in newly formed neural connections (footprints in the snow).

All of this happens without any conscious effort - we have no conscious idea of what is going on in our brains on a neural level. These functions are totally self-organized and keep us alive. Only if something goes wrong (in the case of an illness, for example), we become aware how marvelous the brain really is.

The brain is the most adaptable organ we have. Experiences we make in our daily lives have a significant impact on its inner architecture. The way we think about them forms our identity and shapes our personality.

The only thing the brain cannot do is not to learn. When we are happy, we learn more easily. We must discover for ourselves — no one can do it for us. We can't take a memory stick and download (let's say) *kung fu* in our brain. We must learn, we must train, and we must be coached.

So, learning is essentially an act of self-formation. I use the term *autopoiesis* for this.[4] It means that we build our own perception of the world *in ourselves*. Our senses deliver information about the outside world to the brain. The mind then builds a representation of it inside.

The process of representation is a *construction*. We don't see the world as it is. We only consciously perceive a construction of it. To stick to the previous example, everything I know about *kung fu*, I know because I constructed (or re-constructed) it in my mind.

Scientists still don't know exactly how this works. But somehow, the neural connections we form in our brains correlate to things, situations, and people in the outside world. We experience something and form a corresponding neural pattern, which (somehow) encodes the experience or our memory of it. This is a very active process.

Learning and memory formation are very energy-consuming, active processes. Even if you are seemingly passive — sitting on your couch, listening to music — your brain works *very* hard. Your ears only perceive soundwaves. Your nerves only send electrical impulses to the brain. Only inside your brain, these impulses are recombined and decoded to form the *perception* of music.

To me, it's a miracle.

Important points to remember

✓   Our basic psychological needs offer tremendous opportunities for personal growth.

✓   Exploration is autonomous learning.

✓   There is intentional learning, informal or incidental learning, and implicit learning.

✓   A happy brain likes to learn. If you do something you like, you will learn without any apparent effort (low-key, low-threshold learning).

✓   There are 86 billion neurons in the human brain. How our brains develop depends highly on our surroundings as kids (impoverished – enriched).

✓   Autopoiesis means that we build our own perception of the world in ourselves.

Chapter references

1   Grossmann, Karin; Grossmann, Klaus E. (2012): *Bindungen. Das Gefüge psychischer Sicherheit*. 5. Aufl. Stuttgart: Klett-Cotta.

2   A very interesting article on these numbers: Herculano-Houzel, Suzana (2009): "The Human Brain in Numbers: A Linearly Scaled-up Primate Brain." *Frontiers in Human Neuroscience*, 3, 31.

3   This example is originally from Manfred Spitzer, a German neuroscientist and psychiatrist.

4   From ancient greek: αυτος "self" and ποιεω "to build."

PART 2

The first part of this book has mainly been about laying the ground for what comes next. Now we get into the nitty-gritty of cognitive science, emotion psychology, and stress. All of this will, in turn, be the foundation for part three. In part three, I will talk about my personal take-aways from all this and my tool kit for teaching.

Chapter 8

The Basis of (nearly) Everything: Neurons and Cognition

The brain is amazingly adaptable - it continually changes and reorganizes itself. We go through our daily lives (mostly), having no idea how much is going on inside. Learning takes place all the time; it can be conscious or unconscious, and it can be intentional, informal, or implicit.

This learning shapes the way our brain is interconnected, its very architecture. It also changes our thinking. Neural pathways, which are more often used, are easier to excite. So, what we experience influences our way of thinking, the way we address the world, and how we assess situations.

All this happens based on given brain architecture — everybody has in principle the same brain anatomy. We have typical circuits in our brains, we all have a reward system, we all have memory systems, and we all have emotion centers. Nevertheless, how these structures are shaped in detail is highly personal.

Research has shown that our brain can be changed. The brain's plasticity allows it to adapt very fast to changes in how we think and see the world. (By very fast, I mean in a matter of weeks). If you take part in an eight-week meditation course, your brain will change - the structural changes can be seen in a brain scan. I find that absolutely remarkable, especially given the short period of time.

As humans, we have basic brain structures in common. We also share the same basic needs. How we approach our needs may be highly personal. At the core, we have them in common. We all need to be somewhat in control of our surroundings. We try to avoid pain. We want to feel good about ourselves. And we need significant relationships in our lives.

The individual difference lies in how we think about it (or in fancy scientific terms: *cognition*).

Cognition is our ability to have thoughts, understand, gather knowledge, and experience. Cognition is closely linked to the senses and our memory. We need input through our senses — they provide the building blocks of our internal representation of the world. Memory is also very important. Without memory, we fail to recognize people or situations.

It is really heartbreaking to see when people suffer from memory loss. I've experienced it in my own family. It is (unfortunately) quite common, especially in the elderly. Patients who suffer from Alzheimer's, for example, sometimes forget how to perform basic body motions. They may forget how to swallow or get stuck in a movement and do it again and again (that's called *perseveration*).

So, we cannot overstate the importance of memory for our mind. Actually, everything we talked about so far rests on the fact that we have a mind. The mind is amazing - it encompasses our consciousness, thinking, emotions, and memory, how we perceive ourselves and the world, with how we judge situations and that we have language.[1]

I often wonder why we have a mind in the first place.

Perhaps this comes as a surprise but look at it from a perspective of convenience. The mind keeps us thinking all the time; we brood, speculate, and ponder all day — maybe we would be better off without it? Maybe living on instincts is a better option? Maybe we could avoid a lot of heartache and suffering that way?

If "ignorance is bliss" (as the folk saying goes), maybe mindlessness, having no mind at all, is even more blissful?

As blissful as that might be, having a mind is essential. We have a mind because it serves an evolutionary purpose. Everything in nature (and we humans are part of nature - we tend to forget that too often) is "designed"[2] to help survival. Evolution means that throughout generations, random mutations occur. If they offer advantages, organisms with this special mutation will have more offspring.

Thus, the gene pool changes. Subsequently, the others *without* the mutation are at a disadvantage. They may even die out in the long run. The new genes, which have offered advantages, will become more abundant - this is natural selection. It's a prolonged process but very impactful.

Looking at human beings, we basically carry the same genome with us as our ancestor's hundreds of thousands of years ago.

That in and of itself is mind-boggling.

Think of it - our world has changed so much since then.

Yet if you look just at the last twenty years, the change is astonishing - communication, for example. Twenty years ago, there were fax machines and public phones. Mobile phones were a luxury good - I remember how excited I was to have my first mobile phone! The internet was still in its infancy. Today, we are connected all the time. Talking, tweeting, taking selfies...

If that's a positive change or not, I don't honestly know. It is clear that these recent changes in the world have had a great impact on learning. As we said, the only thing the brain is incapable of is not to learn. Kids nowadays may have worse spelling than prior generations, but they have learned many other skills in the process.

The world we live in is much *noisier*. There is constant background noise, a lot of stimuli competing for our attention. We must cope with a much higher amount of interference than our ancestors. Imagine a person from 300 years ago. Our cities would be unbelievably loud and noisy for him or her - a severe case of over-stimulation.

We, as contemporary humans, have learned to live with it.

We can cope with so much information raining down on us because the brain has powerful defense mechanisms. It weeds out unimportant information, selects the input most interesting to us, and cuts through the noise. Actually, the nervous system does that on several different levels. The effect is that (in the end) only one percent of outside information gets through to us.[3] Evolutionary, ancient brain systems (which we share with a lot of other animals, thus often dubbed the "reptilian brain") take a key role in this process.

When neuroscience started to take off twenty years ago, there was often the misconception that the brain has clear areas devoted to only one thing. Today we know that things are much more complex. The brain is heavily interconnected; many (especially higher) functions of the brain work in circuits. After a stroke, for example, brain areas can cover damaged areas and retain some of the missing functions.

The brain is truly resilient and absolutely remarkable. Its prime focus is to keep us alive and functioning - it does that very well. And to do so, the brain tries to avoid dangers. So you could say the main job of the brain is to *anticipate* dangerous situations. The brain is a great forecaster. It takes its storage of experiences and tries to forecast what is going to happen next.

So, a very important part of getting along with our world is to *recognize patterns*. Every time we see something, we gather information and organize it within our brain. We take the new information and compare it with what we already know. The nerve cells fine-tune themselves - it's an ongoing process and costs a lot of energy.

That's also the reason why the brain does not like change very much. Change means effort. If something changes, the brain needs to adapt. It needs to build new pathways and spend more energy. From an evolutionary perspective, it pays off to be *stingy* energetically.

It pays off to be "conservative" regarding one's energy because you never know what's will happen next. You might need your energy the next minute to flee from a lion or some other mortal danger. It's better to conserve it.

So, every time we learn something new, we change our ideas, or we alter our perspective — that's actually a (small) *miracle*! It's a miracle because it's an effort to change. It consumes energy. It is hard. And as humans, we try to avoid that.

For teaching and learning, change is *essential*. When we learn, our brain changes, our knowledge changes, and our perspectives change. All this requires energy and thus commitment. We only use our limited resources of energy if we feel that it's worthwhile to do so.

When I was a student, the prevailing thought in science was that repetition is the key to learning. The learning methods I was taught (to learn Latin vocabulary, for example) were exactly like that: *repeat, repeat, repeat.* I'm sure you've been through this, also. It's mind-numbing, really.

The way how something is learned is essential for how well we can retrieve the information later.

Today we know that learning through repetition works, but there are better ways. The way *how* something is learned is essential for how well we can retrieve the information later. How something is internalized greatly decides how sustainable the knowledge is, and how we learn determines how usable the information is.

If we learn in a fun way, align with our values and interests, and (yes) using repetition, we can actually learn very fast. And not only fast, but also in a manner which keeps the learned information *present* and *fresh* in our memory.

Our "reptilian brain" has a lot to say in this process. Emotions play an important part in learning, even though emotions in education are a difficult topic. In the relevant literature, the importance of (positive) emotions is often stressed — but not much happens.[4] Certainly, in my own time as a student, teachers had little idea of dealing with the emotional side of teaching. Looking right and left nowadays, I don't feel this has changed much.

In psychology, a lot of research was and is done on the topic of emotions.[5] For a long, long time, emotions were thought of as opposed to thought. Nothing could be further from the truth!

We said that cognition is our ability to have thoughts, understand, gather knowledge, and experience. If that is so, then **emotions are an integral part of our cognitive processes**.

Imagine the following situation: You are looking for a used car. The used car salesman is fishy (sorry for the cliché, nothing against used car salespeople here). You look at the car, and everything looks fine on the surface - the price is kind of okay, the salesman is nice, you get coffee, you haggle, and so forth. Still, you have a bad feeling about the whole thing - something is setting you off. You have a gut-feeling that you shouldn't close the deal.

We have these gut-feelings.

Sometimes we act on them, and sometimes we don't.

Here is what is happening from a cognitive perspective: Our subconscious mind is analyzing the incoming information. It's subconscious, so we don't even realize we are doing that. Our subconscious is in protection mode - it's analyzing the interaction while talking with the salesman. It gathers a lot of information: tone of voice, gestures, facial expressions, the surroundings, the taste of the coffee, everything.

In the end, the result of all this subconscious work enters our conscious mind as a gut-feeling - "Something's fishy here!" Your subconscious raises a red flag. We may be unable to pinpoint exactly what is setting us off, but we have the distinct feeling that we shouldn't buy a car from this man. In scientific terms, we call that a *conscious percept of subconscious cognition.*

You see, emotions are part of our cognitive processes. They serve an essential purpose. Emotions are somatic markers. We should not confuse cognition with *rationality*. (I'm not even sure pure rationality even exists).

The manner of our learning greatly influences how well we learn, and the circumstances we experienced while we were learning have a significant impact. We remember how we felt when we use the skills we have acquired. My teachers often used abusive pedagogy. (Also called "black pedagogy." The term was coined as a reference to "black magic," the magic used by evil wizards in popular culture).

Dark, abusive pedagogy uses stress, anxiety, and over-powering to make people learn. It primarily uses negative reinforcement. If you are not fast enough, you are punished. If you make mistakes, you are punished. If you fail, you are punished.

When I was in the army, there was a motto written on the wall: "If it doesn't kill us, it makes us harder!" From a teaching perspective, that's absolutely wrong: What doesn't kill you makes you *weaker*!

Neuroscience shows that all meaningful experiences leave a trace in the brain. If a situation is bad for us (but we barely make it through), this memory will be kept as a reference for the future. We will remember how we felt - it's a somatic marker. The next time a new situation resembles the stored memory, we will relive the previous situation. We will feel the same. We will go down the anxiety road and be very stressed.

Unfortunately, abusive pedagogy is very common in many fields with high-performance thresholds. You see it a lot in competitive sports, the arts, college, and at schools. Have you seen the movie "Whiplash"? It's about a young man studying drums with an abusive professor. The student tries to please the demands of his professor with total disregard for his own safety. He even accepts intense bodily harm to get in his teacher's good books.

Of course, that's a movie.

But reality is every bit like that.

If you have the stomach for it, you can watch the documentary, "Over the limit."[6] It's about two Russian athletes, rhythmic gymnasts, and how they were trained for the Olympics. You can see first-hand how the coaches use every psychological trick in the book. They punish, they withhold affection, then they show affection again (then the cycle repeats).

It's brutal and hard to watch. It makes you realize how much hardship young people are willing to bear sometimes. They do so to fulfill their dreams (or what they see as their dreams at that point in their lives).

One of the most striking sequences in the documentary is when original footage from the training sessions is shown to one of the athletes. (This took place months after the Olympics). The athlete can't remember *any* of it. It shows how the mind retreated into partial amnesia to protect the personality structure. (This process, *retrograde amnesia,* is actually quite common with victims of shock).

Black pedagogy can be very effective. At least short-term — that's why it is used.

You could argue that the athletes want it themselves! Life is hard; the Olympics are a once-in-a-lifetime opportunity; they win a gold medal in the end. So where's the blame? The problem is that in the long run, there can be quite severe psychological consequences. These consequences can be depression, anxiety attacks, and even suicidal tendencies.

In a recent paper by a French research group around Karine Schaal, the researchers argued that generalized anxiety disorder (GAD) is often found in elite athletes. We speak of GAD only if strong worrying and tension occur over a long period of time - it should not be confused with "normal" levels of worry. If GAD is diagnosed, it means that there is a clinically relevant level of psychological strain.

The degree varies to which athletes have GAD. But those athletes who do aesthetic sports (gymnastics, synchronized swimming and figure skating) are especially vulnerable. This might be the case because in these sports (as in the arts), there is always a certain level of *subjective bias*: If you fail or win is not determined by *objective standards* alone.

If you enter a competition, you depend on the judges to be fair and detach from their own biases. On top of that, it's not only the judges, but your teammates or your coaches' pressure that can be tremendous. Your success heavily depends on how others see your performance. The pressure to be "perfect" is therefore very strong. It seems like this is causing a lot of misery.[7]

In general, perfectionism is on the rise in our society. It's not only confined to sports. Most of us also know this desire to be "perfect." It may be very common but is actually very harmful to our psychological well-being. As Anne Wilson Schaef put it, "Perfectionism is Self-Abuse of the Highest Order".[8]

More on this in the next chapter.

Important points to remember

✓   Cognition is our ability to have thoughts, understand, gather knowledge, and have experiences.

✓   The world we live in offers constant background noise, a lot of stimuli competing for our attention. The brain has strong defense mechanisms against over-stimulation.

✓   The brain is truly resilient; its prime focus is to anticipate dangerous situations, to keep us alive and functioning.

✓   For teaching and learning, behavioral change is essential. How we learn determines how usable given information is. Emotions are an essential part of learning.

✓   Abusive pedagogy is very common in many fields with high-performance thresholds.

Chapter references

1   There is a long discussion throughout the centuries about what constitutes a mind. I would rather skip it here. If you are interested, I recommend McCarthy, Gabby (2018): *Introduction to Metaphysics*. Waltham Abbey: ED-Tech Press.

2   "designed" is set in inverted commas because I mean a process of evolutionary development, not an intentional design effort.

3   See for more information: Schirp, H. (2009): Wie ‚lernt' unser Gehirn Werte und Orientierungen? Herrmann, U. (Hrsg.): *Neurodidaktik. Grundlagen und Vorschläge für gehirngerechtes Lehren und Lernen*, Weinheim und Basel: Beltz

4   Twenty years ago, this was written by Dassler. For reference, see: Dassler, Henning (1999): "Emotion und pädagogische Professionalität: Die Bedeutung des Umgangs mit Gefühlen für sozialpädagogische Berufe".URL:http://digisrv-1.biblio.etc.tu-bs.de:8080/docportal/servlets/MCRFileNodeServlet/DocPortal_derivate_00001104/Document.pdf [25.02.2020].

5   I'm especially fond of the Geneva school; see Scherer, Klaus R. (2005): "What are emotions? And how can they be measured?" *Social Science Information* 44(4), 695–729.

6   You can find the trailer here: https://youtu.be/W47flKJJAVw

7   A good overview of different sports and psychological problems can be found here: Karine Schaal et al. (2011): "Psychological Balance in High Level Athletes: Gender-Based Differences and Sport-Specific Patterns." *PLoS One* 4;6(5):e19007. Although the level of psychological problems is no higher than in the general population in total, there are very interesting statistical deviations in some sports.

8   If you would like to read more from her, I recommend her 2004 book: "Meditations for Women Who Do Too Much."

Chapter 9

"Everything Is Somewhat Lacking": Perfectionism and the Myth of Merit

Perfectionism can be self-abusive. Many people suffer a lot while trying to reach unattainable goals. *Ideals are ideals* — by definition, they are unreachable. Looking to be perfect can lead to harsh self-criticism. It can significantly contribute to anxiety and depression.

There is an amazing study about this, conducted by psychologists Thomas Curran and Andrew Hill. This study looked at the development of perfectionism over the past generations. Curran and Hill interviewed more than 40,000 college students covering a 30-year period.[1]

They found out that the level of perfectionism has increased a great deal over the decades - 33 percent! It seems like this increase goes hand in hand with deep cultural changes. Young people are convinced nowadays that things (and also themselves) should be *perfect*.[2]

Young people (and not only them) view life, society, and the world in total through a *competitive lens*. The idea that the world is ruled by markets and market-driven competition is deeply embedded in today's western culture.

Everything is data. People judge others and themselves by looking at the number of Facebook friends they have, the number of views their YouTube video received, or how many people liked their Instagram post.

Social media have received a lot of criticism recently. In my opinion, a lot of it is justified; some of the critique isn't. Social media can bring together people who share interests in a given area — that's great! Problems develop when there are hidden vulnerabilities beneath the surface. Our brains didn't develop for constant multi-media use, and to find a balanced way between engaging online and living offline is quite a struggle.

In truth, our brains do not multi-task. Rather, they rapidly switch between different actions, which is energy-consuming. Since our ability to pay attention has (rather strong) limits, we must decide what to do next in a fraction of a second.

Modern technology often provides distractions. Our phone pings, and we drop everything else — even if the incoming message, tweet or whatever is objectively *unimportant*. We are conditioned to constantly check our social media. If we fail to do so, we may even feel like we lose something.[3] We feel disconnected. Giving up our devices is not an option, but I strongly recommend a more planned approach towards accessibility.[4]

Distractions are dangerous in the sense that they make the mind unfocused - a wandering mind is an unhappy mind.[5] As humans, we have this amazing quality. We can *afford* to think about what is *not* around us. That's quite an achievement! Unfortunately, this quickly leads to ruminating and mind wandering. These are actually prevalent mind states.

A wandering mind is an unhappy mind — and we are mind-wandering roughly half of the time!

The ability to think about what is not around us has many benefits - we can learn, play, and reflect about things not immediately present in our surroundings. On the one hand, that's wonderful. On the other hand, there is an emotional cost involved. A Harvard study found that indeed a wandering mind is an unhappy mind — and we are mind-wandering roughly half of the time. That's a lot of time, in my opinion!

Social media tends to magnify this problem. Through the media muse, there are always compelling distractions at hand. I can easily choose to be distracted if that's the more exciting thing to do for me at this moment. The design of social media furthers already existing problems. If I have a problem with impulse control, the anonymity of the internet will offer me a field day. I can vent my (negative) emotions all day without having to face any real-life consequences.

That's dangerous. Impulse control is one example; it's likewise with perfectionism. If I need high approval from others, I can foster an image online, which seems perfect. This can get very addictive. Online, it looks like I can achieve what is so unbelievably hard in the real world, to be *perfect*. In the long run, this can be very damaging. If I rely on approval from the outside, I have given away a lot of my power and freedom.

Damage happens when there is no validation from others. When my own carefully groomed online image seems inferior others' self-representation, the result is a depressed mood, psychological problems and a negative self-image. Social media is not evil in and of itself, but when combined with vulnerabilities, it can be dangerous.

Social media strengthens our built-in tendency to judge ourselves and others. We are social animals. We always ask ourselves, "Where am I on the social ladder? What's my position?" But not only that. Whether it's sports, school, or the arts, progress is judged by a metric. This metric is then used to rank people against each other (proficiency tests, for example).

The only applicable metric to judge a person's development are past performances *of this person* - I believe in growth. Growth as a paradigm for teaching makes even literally sense. Seen from the viewpoint of neurobiology, new connections in the brain have to grow to retain a new memory and learn something. So, learning is a process of growth.

Our society, on the other hand, is built on *competition*. That's not inherently bad, but it is important to understand that competition has strong side effects. I like to call these side effects *friction loss*. In mechanics, friction loss is the power you lose when trying to overcome the friction between two objects.

In a motor, you lose a lot of power just to get it going. Similarly, you lose a lot of energy in a system where people compete against each other - much of their energy is spent fighting against others. The energy is lost to the common system. It makes much more sense to invest this power to further a common goal.

We have this false sense of meritocracy. If you work hard, you will get ahead. Recent years have shown that this is not the case. Many factors contribute to your success or failure, and many of them are *absolutely arbitrary*.

There is an excellent book by Robert H. Frank (from Cornell University) on this topic. In his book, he shows that chance opportunities can have a great impact in the long run. Your date of birth, for example! Your birthday is something you *really* have no power over. You are born the day you are born. It seems trivial. But it's not.

Children are grouped in cohorts according to their dates of birth. If the dividing line is (let's say) September 1st, then a child born on August 30th belongs to the former year's class; a child born on September 2nd to the new year's class.

In effect, the first child (born on August 30th) is almost a year younger than the oldest in his or her class. Personal development doesn't follow external schedules. It's safe to assume that (generally speaking) the older children will be stronger physically and more developed mentally.

Subsequently, they are likely deemed more "talented" because of that. They have an inherent advantage just because of their birth dates. Studies have shown that top athletes worldwide have birth dates that cluster in certain months of the year - it's an established phenomenon called the *birthday effect*.

We live in a competitive world. That's a given. What's important to understand is that success within this competition is *not only* driven by hard work and talent. There are also random factors (like the birthday effect), which can translate into significant advantages.

The funny thing is that successful people tend to underestimate the number of random factors contributing to their success; they tend to believe it's all down to their hard work. Of course, without commitment and effort, it's all naught. But there are many other factors as well: your birthday, where you grow up, which school you attend, family connections, networks, and so on. (I haven't even talked about race, sexual orientation, and gender.) In sum, *pure* meritocracy is a myth.[6]

The idea that we simply have to work harder and things will be okay is wrong. It's wrong to think that we'll receive the status and reward we deserve if we strive hard enough. Especially harmful is the mirror image of the idea that if you fail, it's solely because you haven't worked hard enough. You must settle for less *because* you were unwilling to endure enough hardship - this sentiment is wrong. Nevertheless, the internet is full of self-help, "motivation" videos beating this drum.

Think about the psychological ramifications of growing up in a society guided by these mindsets. The prevalent view is that human beings are fundamentally flawed. The societal focus lies on deficiencies and evaluation. In effect, this leads to an emphasis on failure and hypersensitivity to criticism. From a therapy perspective, emphasis on failure and hypersensitivity to criticism is exactly what constitutes a *perfectionist*.

Although, there is a distinction to be made. There are nuances between a healthy sense of wanting to achieve discipline and perfectionism. The main difference is the question, "Is there personal suffering?" Perfectionists suffer a great deal.

Perfectionism leads to social isolation and inactivity. Inactivity may sound surprising, but it's not. You can see it frequently with *writer's block*. If you are preoccupied with writing the *perfect sentence*, chances are you will not write a single sentence at all. Doing something is a confrontation with our own deficiencies. We always lack something.

Perfectionists cannot bear this feeling of being deficient; for them, it feels better to do nothing at all. Through inactivity, they try to avoid confrontation with their deficiencies. They hope to reduce their pain by not exposing themselves.

The problem is that avoidance tends to multiply our misery. It makes sense - if we avoid something and feel *situational relief*, then this behavior is reinforced. I still remember the first day I played at the Vienna State Opera. It was only a rehearsal, but while riding on the tram to the opera, I felt so bad in my stomach that I thought I had to throw up, and I earnestly toyed with the thought to turn around and call in sick. (I didn't in the end, I'm still proud of that!)

If I had given in to the sentiment, chances are that I would have done it the next time too. We feel subjectively better now, so we tend to go down that road again and again. In the end, we have more problems, not less. Our anxiety gets stronger.

From my point of view, it's most important to understand that failure is not being weak. We need self-worth, which doesn't hinge on outperforming others. Outside approval is essentially overrated, and unfortunately, it's also psychologically pervasive.

Evaluation is all around. We are accustomed to judging our worth through approval from others. You see it everywhere: at school, during exam time and at the workplace when being evaluated. In sports, the arts, and online. For perfectionists, there is ample opportunity to worry and to bathe in self-doubt.

In these situations, perfectionists fear that they won't be able to perform up to their standards. That's bad because they fear their (perceived) weaknesses will be made public. Their innermost frailties will become apparent. This thought is unbearable to them. You can imagine how much stress this is, both physically and psychologically, and may lead to severe health problems.

As a classical musician, I know perfectionism very well. It's hard to get out of it. To me, it seems key to reconcile with oneself. Perfectionism means that we suffer from the gap between our *ideal* and *reality*. If we can reconcile ourselves with ourselves, we can be more compassionate. Compassion always starts with self-compassion, I'm sure of that.

It's also crucial to re-examine goals. We can strive for perfection, but maybe it's healthier to redefine it. Rather than perfection, we could aim for *mastery*. We could be proud of our diligence and our perseverance, focusing on the process more. Ultimately, the process of achieving something is more meaningful than the goal.

The process is more important than the goal because *better is good*.[7] From a pragmatic viewpoint, a *better* result is better than no result and better than the previous result. If you wait for a perfect result, you will likely wait forever - perfectionism tends to lead to postponing. The mind of the perfectionist says, If you don't start, you cannot fail!

Perfectionism fosters paralysis. This paralysis often goes together with negative reflection and rumination. Impatience, hard self-critique, and demands won't help. This is why I always advocate mental hygiene. Be cautious about what you ingest psychologically; it will impact you.

Vulnerabilities can be found on both sides of the classroom. You may be perfectionistic, critiquing yourself most harshly, or your students might be perfectionists, trying to project a perfect image online and suffering from it.

I'm writing this because mental disorders, anxiety, stress, and depression are on the rise. I think there are reasons why this is the case, and perfectionism is one of them - social media use and the overall shape of our society and economic system is another. When you teach, please keep these statistics in mind. Know that some of your students may suffer from rather severe health disorders, like depression, stress, and anxiety, even if it doesn't seem so from the outside.[8]

Important points to remember

✓ Perfectionism can be self-abusive. Many people suffer while trying to reach unattainable goals.

✓ We are social animals. Social media strengthens our built-in tendency to judge ourselves and others.

✓ Our society is built on competition. Competition has strong side effects.

✓ Successful people tend to underestimate the number of random factors contributing to their success. Pure meritocracy is a myth.

✓ Mental hygiene is crucial. Be cautious about what you ingest psychologically.

Chapter references

1   Curran, T., & Hill, A. (2019): "Perfectionism Is Increasing Over Time: A Meta-Analysis of Birth Cohort Differences From 1989 to 2016". *Psychological Bulletin*, 145, 410–429.

2   Here is Curran's great TED-talk on the topic: https://www.youtube.com/watch?v=IFG1b1-EsW8

3   In psychology, this is called *reactance*. Reactance is the "motivation to regain freedom after it has been lost or threatened" (Steindl et al, 2015).

4   For more information on this topic, please refer to Gazzaley, A., & Rosen, L.D. (2016): *The Distracted Mind: Why Technology Hijacks Our Brain and How to Enhance Our Focus Amidst the Noise*. Cambridge, Massachusetts: MIT Press.

5   This is the title of the following very interesting article: Killingsworth, Matthew A., Gilbert, Daniel T. (2010): "A Wandering Mind Is an Unhappy Mind." *Science*, Vol. 330, Issue 6006, pp. 932.

6   I highly recommend Robert H. Frank's book for further reading: *Success and luck. Good fortune and the myth of meritocracy*.

7   This saying goes famously back to President Obama.

8   For depression, here is the official website of the WHO: https://www.who.int/news-room/fact-sheets/detail/depression

Chapter 10

Living in the Urban Jungle:
Stress, Survival Mode and Self-efficacy

Mental disorders, anxiety, stress, depression are on the rise: Let's have a closer look. Maslow located "physiological" needs (food, water, warmth, rest) at the bottom of his pyramid. On the next layer are "safety" needs: That we feel we are free of immediate danger. We need to feel secure.

Besides physiological safety, there is psychological safety. We need a social safety net, psychologically. The social interactions we have, imprint themselves in our brain. The experiences we make form our belief systems and our expectations for the future. Attachment theory calls that *internal working models* - we establish working models of the outer world and compare new experiences to our stored beliefs.

Imagine you are unemployed and looking for a job. You are writing applications, searching online for new job offers, and going to job interviews. At first, you are optimistic and highly motivated. The longer the process takes, the harder it is on you psychologically, and in the end, you may go to a job interview expecting failure already — because you had to endure so much of it in the past.

The way we interact with each other forms our experiences and then our *expectations*. In the case of abusive pedagogy, we see how closely linked neural and social interactions are. If you are mistreated for a sufficiently long time, you don't expect to be treated any better. You might even feel okay with it because you never experienced otherwise.

For proper learning, it is very important to be able to modulate stress levels. As a teacher, you must reduce *your own* stress (more on how to achieve that later). You must also be able to relax your students and lessen *their* anxiety and *their* stress.

There are people who advocate "tough love." They say, "Life is not a picnic! We must prepare youngsters for hardship! We must be hard on them to make them tough!" You have no idea how often I hear such sentiments. There are different degrees to it, but this philosophy is very strongly embedded in the minds of many people in education.

I absolutely agree - life is not a picnic.

I can assure the advocates of "tough love" that people have enough hardship in their lives. You don't have to worry about toughening someone up — life will see to that, I promise. If you look at the number and the level of problems the younger generations face today (climate crisis, inequality, economic stagnation, to name a few), you immediately understand that they need *additional support*, not extra pressure.

Please don't get me wrong; this does not mean constant cuddling.

I want to be very clear - support means to offer assistance if needed, *secure attachment*. Support means to refrain from projecting your own deficiencies on the learner. It doesn't mean insulating others from pain. As we have seen, avoidance behavior is ultimately futile and isn't beneficial psychologically.

If we can agree on this, we already accomplished a lot.

The point is that anxiety disorders, stress, and depression are becoming more and more prevalent in our society. A study by the World Health Organization (WHO) found that the number of depressions is worldwide on the rise. In 2015, approximately 322 million people were suffering from depression, 4,4 percent of the global population - 18 percent more than ten years ago.[1]

Learners need support. People may disagree for political or cultural reasons ("tough love"), but the scientific evidence is there. If you look into neuroscience, you see that neural pathways get stronger when they are activated often.

Connections grow thicker, and the thicker the connections, the easier it is to go down that path. This is why stressful experiences lead to *more stress*. Dense neural connections are more easily activated than thin ones. If you have a lot of stress, you gain strong neural correlations, which makes experiencing stress in the future more likely.

The experiences we make shape our brain, and then these engrained experiences influence our perceptions, how we see the world. If I've grown up with abusive learning, I have deeply embedded beliefs. They might be, "Life is hard," "progress is slow," "learning means suffering," "I'm not good enough," etc. All these beliefs actually make learning and overall progress harder. They do not help.

Why not dispense with them altogether? And safe the energy?

There are factors in learning which make learning harder (inhibitive factors). Other factors make learning easier. Inhibitive factors are conditions and circumstances, which block normal brain processes, so that no (or much less) new connections can be formed in the brain.

These blockages can have several reasons; the most prominent among them is *anxiety*. When we are anxious, the brain reduces its learning activity. Or, to be more precise, it refocuses its attention on avoiding danger, sidestepping immediate threats, and ensuring survival.

If a hungry lion comes at you, you don't stop to have a look at the beautiful scenery — you just run!

Think of it this way: If a hungry lion comes at you, you don't stop to have a look at the beautiful scenery — you just run (or you might fight or freeze) - the same with the brain. If you are under a perceived threat (it doesn't matter if the threat is "real" or not), brain functioning is considerably changed. The brain goes into survival mode.

In our modern world, threats are much different than what our ancestors encountered. For them, it might have been the immediate mortal danger of wild beasts, other humans, etc. For us, it's overwhelmingly psychological. We fear job loss, being lonely, old age, long-term illness, speaking in public, things like that.

If you have to speak in public and are anxious about it, you know deep down that you are *not* in mortal danger. No one is going to die if you fail. It will (certainly) be embarrassing or have repercussions on you professionally, but there is no threat to your life. The funny thing is this knowledge does not help!

The body reactions we have when we fear public speaking are more or less the same as the ones our distant ancestors showed when fleeing wild beasts. We try to get along in a modern world with the body and the mental reactions of humans of a very different time. Sometimes, when I'm nervous before an important meeting or going on stage, I remember this - first of all, we are primates, who just happen to wear suits sometimes. Isn't that funny?

If we encounter high stress or perceived threats, we go into survival mode. Later, when the situation has passed, we use the memory of this instance as a reference. This is why it's so important *how we come out* of a dangerous situation and why it's vital how we judge and remember it in retrospect.

It's a big difference to your self-esteem if you *master* a difficult situation or if you have the feeling you *barely* made it through. Here, teaching is absolutely critical. As teachers, our responsibility is immense:

- Firstly, we must *prepare* students so that they can manage tasks ahead of them.
- Secondly, we must design tasks in a ladder-type *climb of difficulty*.
- Finally, we must evaluate the results afterward together, trying to shape the reference memory.

The last point is key. If the student exits a difficult situation with positive feelings, self-esteem, and confidence, self-efficacy will be boosted. Self-efficacy means that we trust that we can reach a certain goal - it's the belief *in* and a personal judgment of our abilities.

If we trust that we can act and use our abilities to fulfill a goal we find worthwhile, we have high self-efficacy. The name and the concept are from psychologist Albert Bandura, who first published a paper on this.[2]

I find the concept of self-efficacy beautiful - it can explain a lot. For example, I always wondered why very talented, highly gifted people could quite suddenly fail under stress. I think it is because of a lack of self-efficacy. They may be talented, hard-working, and highly intelligent, but perhaps deep down, they don't really trust in their abilities. Or maybe they have belief systems, which keep them from really fulfilling their potential.

As a teacher, I see that a lot.

I think that it is our highest duty as teachers to try to promote self-efficacy in students. Again, this does not mean constant cuddling. Self-efficacy implies that we *have* abilities in the first place. And abilities need to be gained, to be honed, and to be used.

Important points to remember

✓ The experiences we make form our belief systems and our expectations for the future (internal working models).

✓ For proper learning, it is very important to be able to modulate stress levels. Learners need support.

✓ Neural pathways get stronger when they are activated often. When we are anxious, the brain reduces its learning activity.

✓ We try to get along in a modern world with the body and the mental reactions of humans of a prehistoric age.

✓ If students exit a difficult situation with positive feelings, self-esteem, and confidence, self-efficacy is boosted. Self-efficacy is the belief that we can use our competencies to impact a given situation and reach a goal.

Chapter references

1   Here is the study: Depression and Other Common Mental Disorders: Global Health Estimates. Geneva: World Health Organization; 2017.

2   The seminal paper on the subject can be found here: Bandura, Albert (1982). "Self-efficacy mechanism in human agency." *American Psychologist*. 37 (2): 122–147. doi:10.1037/0003-066X.37.2.122.

Chapter 11
Anxiety and Stress Reduction

When we are in (mortal) danger, we don't stop to look at the scenery. When we are anxious, the brain focuses on getting rid of the anxiety-provoking situation - there's not much energy left for *learning*. In retrospect, when we look back on the situation, we may have learned something. (For example, "I can now perform under stress" or "lots of fast food combined with roller coaster rides spell disaster!") But that happens *afterward*. In the anxiety-provoking situation itself, we generally just want to overcome it or flee.

Anxiety itself is actually something positive. Whenever I say that in a seminar, eyebrows shoot up. If you tell an anxious person that anxiety is positive, the person might even feel insulted. You will most likely not achieve anything. But it's true - anxiety has positive aspects. We tend to see anxiety as something negative, because it is connected with unpleasant body sensations. It generates a general feeling of stress and leads to overall poorer performance.

Anxiety is an emotion - it serves as a somatic marker. It labels a situation as "dangerous" or "challenging." The anxiety itself wakes up our body (and our mind as well) and tells us, "Your attention is needed here!" The body reacts to anxiety-provoking situations by releasing chemicals, which sharpen our responses.

This happens through a complex system of feedback and connections called the HPA axis (the hypothalamic-pituitary-adrenal axis). It has three parts: the hypothalamus (important for memory), the pituitary gland ("sitting" below the thalamus like a pea), and the adrenal glands (on top of both kidneys).

These three organs and the way they interact control stress reactions. They also regulate many other processes in the body. When I first learned about it, I was amazed at how many processes the HPA is involved in - the immune system, sexuality, digestion, moods, and emotions.

It is not surprising then that stress affects all these processes - they are linked through the HPA. If you are very stressed, your digestion might be off, and you (most likely) will not be interested in sex. You may have mood swings, and your immune system will not be working at its best.

Under stress, your body's defense systems are less useful. You are more vulnerable to getting sick. That's the reason why so many people catch a cold when they are stressed.

Catching a cold is one thing, but stress over long periods of time has a major negative impact on health. This is because the stress system and the immune system do not work at the same time. They alternate over the course of day and night. In science, this is called a "circadian biorhythm."[1]

The stress system is most active during the early morning hours (4-6 am) and then again, but less so in the afternoon (around 4 pm). The immune system works exactly the other way around. It has its peak in the late afternoon and during the night.

If you face unresolvable differences in relationships with others, suffer from chronic stress, or are depressed, your immune system can't work properly. It doesn't respond correctly to threats. This dampened, curbed immune response can cause of a number of health problems, including chronic *fatigue*. Many scientific studies show that long periods of stress lead to negative consequences for brain functioning, brain structure, and aging processes.

Aging is a fascinating topic. Did you know that your brain can regenerate? That you can get new brain cells? When I was a student, it was common knowledge that humans do not produce new nerve cells when they are older. Today we know that this is false.

We can add up to 700 new nerve cells a day to our hippocampus (an area crucial for memory). That may not sound like much — compared to the 86 million neurons we have in the brain, but think about it - if you get 700 new cells per day, you have a "new" hippocampus by the age of fifty![2]

That's obviously good news.

Unfortunately, there is a catch. If you're stressed or anxious for a long time, you won't grow new nerve cells. And not only that, stress reduces your general life expectancy. Stress makes you die sooner, and your risk of suffering a stroke is higher.[3] You're more vulnerable to infections, and if you suffer from a condition like asthma, diabetes, arthritis, even multiple sclerosis — all these are made worse by stress.

As you can see, anxiety and stress greatly impact on our health and our lives in general. Anxiety in itself is not bad. But the anxiety we consciously feel is only the tip of the iceberg. There are a lot of processes beneath the surface of our consciousness. We may have a lot of *background anxiety*, anxiety below the threshold of consciousness, without even knowing it!

Anxiety is an emotion. When we can sense it, then it is a feeling. How do we measure it? How can we compare my level of anxiety to yours? One possibility is to look at the level of stress hormones in the bloodstream. The other is to see in a brain scan how active brain structures connected to anxiety are. First and foremost, that's the amygdala.

The amygdala is a structure deep within the brain. Early scientists (with a lot of fantasy) found that its shape resembled an almond, thus the name "amygdala" (greek for almond). All the more complex animals have an amygdala (or rather two, one on each side of the brain). The amygdala is part of the limbic system and is mostly concerned with emotional responses, gauging memories, and making decisions.

Now it gets really interesting. If you look at the amygdala's size and connectivity, you can predict the degree of anxiety someone has in daily life. Everybody has anxiety - that's simply a fact. But if you look at the brain structures involved, you see a lot of individual differences. Keeping in mind that the brain strengthens pathways often used, that's not very surprising, right?

If I'm anxious most of the time, then these "highways" in the brain will become broader, stronger, and easier to access. The good news is that it's not a one-way street. If I change my every-day life, I can reduce my anxiety and the size and density of my amygdala.

Recently, researchers found out that we must distinguish between how we feel when we are anxious and conscious *awareness*.[4] Scientists can show you a picture, for example, without your consciousness knowing it. This is called a "masked stimulus." If they show you a picture that makes you fearful, your body will react.

You will show all the signs of anxiety — heart beating faster, sweaty palms, you name it — without feeling anxiety consciously. It sounds crazy, but that's how it is! Maybe your consciousness will then say, "Hey, I sense anxiety; there must be some reason for it. So let's get anxious," but that's coming later. Initially, you don't have conscious fear. Actually, that's quite similar to the gut feelings we spoke about earlier.

As I said, this is a complex system of feedback and mutual influences. The important point is to keep in mind that the amygdala is very good at evaluating threats. It's active if there is something in our environment that might pose a threat to our well-being and is heavily connected with other regions of the brain. Together they regulate emotion and modulate perception.

A study done by researchers from Stanford found out that children who experience a lot of anxiety have larger amygdalas; they are much more likely to suffer from depression and anxiety disorders later when they are adults. It even looks like stressful experiences *during pregnancy* can have an impact:[5] Children of mothers who suffered a lot of stress during pregnancy are more vulnerable to stress after birth.

There is a lot of research done in neuroscience. How *exactly* anxiety and stress change the brain connections is not yet known.[6] I find the brain's ability to change and re-organize absolutely miraculous. It never stops to amaze me that our brain can grow differently according to what we experience. For me, the conclusion is clear -we must shape our experiences in beneficial ways. If we can re-organize our brains, we must make sure that we give it the *best input*.

The one thing I love most about science is that you always test things. It's not enough to say that this and that is good for you. You need to be able to test it. If you can't test it, then it's not science.

There is scientific evidence that if we "feed" our brain with good input, then the areas associated with stress will shrink. In a study, participants reported that they experienced less stress if they took part in a stress reduction program. You may think, "Big deal — of course, they will report less stress! They know they are supposed to feel less stress. It's a stress reduction program after all!"

That's true.

(And that's also the reason why self-reporting is always extremely unreliable.)

But when these participants were scanned, their brains showed significant shrinkage in the density of the amygdala.[7] It was not only that they felt better subjectively; their brains had changed due to psychological exercises. It is true, our minds profoundly influence our bodies.

You can alter your brain by solely thinking in a specific manner. That's pretty amazing, isn't it?

If our minds influence our bodies, how should we go about it? What then is good input?

The participants of the study I just mentioned completed an eight-week course in Mindfulness-based Stress Reduction (MBSR). After eight weeks, changes were already visible in their brain scans. Imagine that - you have a lifetime of habits, of thinking patterns deeply ingrained in your brain. You can achieve demonstrable changes, changes you can see in an fMRI scan, within eight weeks.

We have deeply ingrained thought patterns. Habits are typical responses we have to situations around us. They develop by repetition. In the same situation, we do the same thing: If you come home from work and turn on the TV for a sufficient period of time, you will form a habit. That in and of itself is neither good nor bad.

When we have a strong habit energy, we don't think. We just do it! We may not even be consciously aware of what we are doing. As the saying goes, "First we form habits, then they form us."[8] The good news is that your habits can change. *You* can change your habits. I don't say it's easy, but it's possible.[9]

If we want to change our habits (physical or mental), we must first acknowledge that we have them. Then we have to initiate something new, a new behavior, in order to replace the old one. This needs many repetitions until we reach automaticity. To get there, old behavior patterns need to be disrupted. The personal environment needs to be changed. It's very hard to change behavior if all the surroundings stay the same.[10]

This is precisely what a course like MBSR tries to achieve. Eight weeks may sound like little to change a deeply ingrained behavior pattern — actually, it's a pretty good period of time to form new habits.[11] In studies, it took participants between 18 to 254 days to establish a new habit. A wide range! To develop a new habit it is fundamental to repeat a behavior consistently; with repetition, automaticity will increase. If you miss one opportunity to perform your new habit, it doesn't harm the process. But ultimately, consistency is key.

Consistency is important because it will change your brain structure - you can alter the way you think. In turn, this will change the plasticity of your brain. Because of that, meditation is good for you. I'm especially fond of MBSR since it is *independent of any religion*. I find religious overtones rather harmful in this regard. There might be people who would like to have less stress and learn a technique to do so, but they are fine with their religion (or having no religion) — they simply don't want to become yogis or Buddhists.

That's why I think it's so important to say this - it has nothing to do with religion. You can practice meditation regardless of your persuasion. Mindfulness meditation comes from the Buddhist tradition, but the MBSR system initiated by Jon Kabat-Zinn has no religious overtones. Kabat-Zinn says the practice of mindfulness means merely to purposefully focus your attention.[12]

In meditation, you focus on the present moment and try not to judge. That may not sound like much: In truth, it is amazingly hard. (Especially the non-judgemental part).

You focus on the present moment and try not to judge. That may not sound like much, but in truth, it is amazingly hard. (Especially the non-judgemental part). If you try it, you will see that we as humans judge all the time! I'm also absolutely convinced that we are *trained* to judge all the time. We always try to distinguish whether this is good for me or bad? What's the endgame? What's the other person's agenda? What do I get out of this situation! And so forth.

In recent years, a lot of research has been done on the topic of mindfulness meditation. Scientists are especially interested in finding ways to help patients suffering from depression, anxiety, stress, or pain through mindfulness. Lately, it was discovered that mindfulness meditation not only reduces your stress but also diminishes cell aging.[13]

These effects do not come through an eight-week course. The people studied here were long-term meditators - they meditated regularly and did so from 5 to 38 years. What I find interesting is that they lived normal lives apart from that (family, career, hobbies). They were not monks in a cave or sages from the Himalayas.

Additional studies show the benefit of meditation for other things, for example, your immune system. That's not surprising since stress impacts your immune system negatively. If you reduce stress, your immune system benefits. What I find remarkable is that these are scientific findings. They are not some ideas or ideologies. They were tested and found to be correct. That makes a huge difference to me — and I hope to you also.

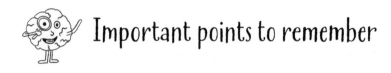 # Important points to remember

✓   Anxiety itself is actually something positive.

✓   Under stress, the body's defense systems are less useful. Long periods of stress lead to negative consequences for brain functioning, brain structure, and aging processes.

✓   Growing new nerve cells (neurogenesis) is possible.

✓   If you look at the amygdala's size and connectivity, you can predict the degree of anxiety someone has in daily life.

✓   We can re-organize our brains. We must shape our experiences in beneficial ways.

✓   Mindfulness means to purposefully focus your attention. You focus on the present moment and try not to judge.

Chapter references

1   See Bauer (2010) for more information on the biology of these processes.

2   An awesome TED-Talk on this topic by neuroscientist Sandrine Thuret can be found here: https://www.youtube.com/watch?v=B_tjKYvEzil

3   A very interesting study on this topic: Jood, K., Redfors, P., Rosengren, A., Blomstrand, C., & Jern, C. (2009): "Self-perceived psychological stress and ischemic stroke: a case-control study." *BMC medicine*, 7, 53.

4   For more on this matter, see: LeDoux, Joseph (2016): *Anxious: Using the Brain to Understand and Treat Fear and Anxiety*. New York, NY: Penguin Random House.

5   Coussons-Read, Mary (2013): "Effects of prenatal stress on pregnancy and human development: Mechanisms and pathways." *Obstetric Medicine: The Medicine of Pregnancy*, 6, 52-57.

6   Warren SL, Zhang Y, Duberg K, et al. (2020): "Anxiety and Stress Alter Decision-Making Dynamics and Causal Amygdala-Dorsolateral Prefrontal Cortex Circuits During Emotion Regulation in Children." *Biol Psychiatry*. 2020; S0006-3223(20)30100-1.

7   The full study can be found here: Hölzel BK, Carmody J, Evans KC, et al. (2010): "Stress reduction correlates with structural changes in the amygdala." *Soc Cogn Affect Neurosci*.;5(1):11-17.

8   Attributed to Rob Gilbert.

9   A fascinating book in this regard is: Doty, James R. (2016): Into the Magic Shop: *A Neurosurgeon's Quest to Discover the Mysteries of the Brain and the Secrets of the Heart*. New York: Avery. I recommend it deeply.

10   I recommend this excellent paper for further reading: Lally, P., & Gardner, B. (2013): "Promoting habit formation." *Health Psychology Review*, 7, 137 - 158.

11   Lally, P., Jaarsveld, C.V., Potts, H., & Wardle, J. (2010): "How are habits formed: Modelling habit formation in the real world." *European Journal of Social Psychology*, 40, 998-1009.

12   More on this here: Kabat-Zinn J. (2003): "Mindfulness-based interventions in context: past, present, and future." *Clin. Psychol.-Sci. Practice* 144–156.

13   A truly exciting study: Laneri, D., Schuster, V., Dietsche, B., Jansen, A., Ott, U., & Sommer, J. (2016): "Effects of Long-Term Mindfulness Meditation on Brain's White Matter Microstructure and its Aging." *Frontiers in aging neuroscience*, 7, 254.

Chapter 12

"Where Does the Stress Come from?" — Stress and Symbiotic Relationships

We have seen that stress impacts the immune system. We have also seen that stress can be reduced by changing your habitual thinking patterns, for example, through MBSR or meditation in general. Scientific, empirical findings back this up.

In recent decades, psychologists worked hard to have a broader data basis on to base their theories. One of the most influential scientists in this regard is Richard Lazarus. Throughout his career, he pressed forward for a better empirical foundation in psychology.[1] Like Bowlby and Ainsworth in attachment theory, he continually worked for reliable data. His main theme was *stress* and how we cope with it.

Learning or being in situations that require learning is a stress to the body system. We do things; we feel things; we react to things. We struggle to push for our interests. We need to adapt to changing circumstances. We must cope with adversity. We think about our environment, and we evaluate it. All this amounts to stress.

The internal evaluation of situations is called *appraisal*. We appraise situations, especially regarding their *level of threat* towards us. We need strategies in order to cope with demanding situations and ever-changing surroundings. We evaluate situations, and this evaluation influences the emotion we consequently feel.

If you think back to my story (being on my way to the opera for the first time as a player), this makes sense. I evaluated my professional situation subconsciously and was very unsure whether I could cope with it. The result was intense anxiety. This is a topsy-turvy approach. Normally, we like to think there is *first* the emotion and *then* the evaluation. But (as Lazarus argues), it's exactly the opposite! We evaluate *first*, and *then* there is the emotional response.

Our needs and motivations greatly guide the way how we appraise a given situation. We ask ourselves, "In which way does this situation matter to me?" If a situation is highly relevant for our needs and motivation, the emotions felt will be strong.[2]

Imagine you love cars. You own a wonderful car, which is the joy of your heart. If some hormone-driven juvenile ruffian scratches the whole side of your car with a key, your emotional response will be very strong because the car means so much to you. On the other hand, if your car is just a means of transport to you, you might not care very much! Motivational relevance influences the emotional intensity of your reaction.

The same is the case if the situation is aligned with your goals or not. You ask yourself, "Does this situation conform to my goals?" Imagine you love doughnuts. You are in a foreign city, craving a good old-fashioned donut. You wander around for ages — finally, you see a doughnut shop. And it's open! What a joy! You wouldn't have felt the same joy seeing an open butcher's or (let's say) a library, so alignment with your goals is essential for the emotional response.

We evaluate situations: This evaluation consequently influences the emotion we feel.
Walking to the opera house, I didn't feel up to the challenge - therefore, I was extremely anxious.

With difficult situations, it is more complicated. When facing adversity, we evaluate which tools we have at our disposal to cope with it quickly. We also try to figure out who is responsible for the mess we are in. We have three different routes we can take:

- Blaming another person (negative)
- Giving credit to someone (positive) or
- Attributing a situation to chance (neutral)
- The route we choose changes how we react.

We take a quick inventory - the tools we have at our disposal determine whether we feel stress or not. If we can solve the problem quickly and easily, it is merely a nuisance. Therefore, the emotions we feel in any given situation are influenced by our judgment of how *easy* it will be to solve the problem. If our resources are lacking, we will feel stressed.

We can cope with this stress in two ways - we can try to alter the situation or change our approach towards it. In the very essence, this is the core of many psychotherapeutic interventions and also of ancient meditation techniques - to accept a situation that cannot be changed or avoided and to try to influence your own appraisal of this (negative) situation, making it less stressful to you.

The beauty of Lazarus' model is that researchers can try to *predict* emotional responses. This is very much like attachment theory, which allows for making prospective statements based on attachment style. I think the gold standard of science is to be able to make reasonable predictions.

If we assess how a person sees and appraises a situation, we can predict how this person will feel about it. A great example is anger. If you are (1) sure someone else is responsible for a bad situation, (2) feel the situation goes against your motivations, and (3) that it is relevant to you — you will (most likely) get angry.

Anxiety, on the contrary, works a bit differently. With anxiety, blame is not administered easily. Maybe I'm to blame, maybe someone else is, or perhaps it's due to prevailing circumstances. Apart from blame, motivations are crucial. To become anxious, the present situation has to *touch my motivations* - I must somehow care. If I see that I have insufficient resources to cope with a situation, anxiety will ensue.

Within the scientific community, there has been some discussion whether an appraisal is a *structure* or a *process*. I personally lean towards the process idea. I do so for the simple reason that I think that *behavior always happens in a sequence*. There is always a cognitive component to it.

There is some cognition involved in leading to an appraisal. I find these underlying cognitive operations most interesting. They can account for *repression*, for example. The mind tends to mask what it fears to confront.[3] Thoughts, ideas, and impulses, which we find taxing, may be repressed to keep the mind from suffering. Freud and Jung have focused on this a lot. Jung speaks of the *shadow*, which gathers in itself everything we refuse to acknowledge about ourselves.[4] The shadow — although repressed — will influence us from its position beneath the surface.

As I said, the cognitive element is key to how we assess a situation. It may be conscious or unconscious, but it will affect how we perceive our reality. Belgian researchers have found that our *thoughts* make emotions last much longer; they are "fuel to the fire."[5] This is why our thoughts matter so much — and the good news is that we can change the way we think!

We inherit many traits and belief systems from other people - our parents, friends, and colleagues. Most of it will happen unconsciously. We form beliefs about ourselves based on the experiences we have. For example, I was always convinced that being nervous automatically leads to a bad performance.

Since being nervous is absolutely the norm for people acting publicly, this belief naturally tended to reduce my performance level. Through much work, I was able to change this belief. Now I believe that it is possible to feel anxious and to perform well at the same time. What a relief!

This is a relatively harmless example. In my practice as a teacher and as a counselor, I encounter many people who suffer a great deal. Mostly, it cannot be detected from the outside - emotional suffering can take place without many people noticing it. Often, the suffering is the result of deeply engrained experiences with significant others. It can happen inside the family, at the workplace, or at school.

Science tells us that the most impressionable period in a person's life is early childhood - the environment imprints itself firmly into the psyche in those years. In this period, beliefs, assumptions about oneself, and thought patterns are established, which tend to influence the whole life.

As children, we live in constant fear of being *abandoned*. This is because we are born "too early" for our development, and we need a social structure to keep us fed, warm, and (generally) alive. As kids, we are ego-centered. We believe that everything has to do with us. This belief makes evolutionary sense since we depend on others to take care of us.

Suppose a child experiences any kind of situation which could be seen as abandonment. In that case, they will become overly stressed (because kids don't have the necessary resources to cope with the situation). Ego-centered by nature, the child will also seek to blame him or herself, searching for the cause of the experience in something they have done or said.

As a parent, I can assure you that every child makes — best intentions notwithstanding — abandonment experiences. That's simply a fact of life. We are imperfect people living in an imperfect world.

Kids will inevitably have abandonment experiences. The vital matter is how they cope with it and which beliefs and mental patterns are already in place to protect against serious harm being inflicted. The ego-centered belief that I (as the kid) am responsible for being abandoned is wrong. Still, although being an inaccurate view, this is the only way a child can interpret what's happening in a meaningful way - it's the only available interpretation to make sense of the world.

When we grow up, we carry these experiences with us. Some therapists call that the *inner child*:[6] This inner child represents of our early experiences, informing and guiding (often subconsciously) our actions and thoughts.

We live in an imperfect world. Even our best intentions do not guarantee that we don't harm other people. We might not mean to, but still, we do. At other times, we might even intend to harm. Or we rationalize our behavior in a way, which allows us to do emotionally harmful things to others while being convinced of serving their best interests. I call that the *rationalization engine within*.

The *rationalization engine within* can lead to emotional atrocities born out of projection, confusion, and anxiety. We tend to inflict harm on the people most close to us. We do so simply because they are close, there is ample opportunity, and we know them so well. If a stranger on the street slanders me, I don't really care - I might suspect some sort of medical condition. But if a person close to me says harmful things, it will hurt me.

Close relationships always carry the danger and the possibility of *harm*. By entering relationships, we make ourselves very *vulnerable*. The teacher-student-relationship is such a case, which is why we (as teachers) have so much responsibility for the students entrusted in our care.

Our responsibility is great - the shadow of a condescending smile at the wrong moment or a wrongly interpreted gesture can be *devastating*. A simple word can implode a student's self-esteem. We must always keep in mind that an off-handedly spoken side remark can greatly impact on the other person's psyche.[7]

We like to think positively about ourselves. Nevertheless, I'm astonished every time I look deeply into my motivations; I see then that they are sometimes not as pure as I would like. It takes a lot of courage to acknowledge that we are not always acting in good faith. Sometimes we harm others with intention.

The closer the relationship, the more opportunity and knowledge to hit the other person most effectively - you know where to apply pressure in order to obtain the "best" results.

It is a big taboo in pedagogy to talk about the *dark side* of educational relationships. I'm not even talking about behavior outside the legal boundaries. I'm talking about *everyday abusive behavior.*

We tend to look at abuse as physical abuse in the first place. While this is correct and indeed the best starting point, I would like to widen the circle further. Everyday emotional abuse leaves no trace. There is no physical evidence, and yet it can be immensely harmful to the individual.

There are many kinds of abusive behaviors - not sharing important information, saying harmful things, manipulation, coercive behavior, you name it. Schnarch remarked that we all have a primitive, punitive, and petty side to us.[8] I think that is true. He also pointed out that this "dark side" gets more prevalent the more two people are "fused" in their relationship.

I think that's the greatest task we face as teachers, but also as parents, spouses, friends - to allow *proximity without fusion* and to accept *vulnerability without lashing out* for the sake of self-protection.

Teacher-student relationships are ideally long-term: it's an investment on both sides. In order to really make an impact, you need a solid basis. This basis is built through many interactions (hopefully good ones). Because we remember how a person behaved in the past, we make reasonable assumptions about their future behavior.

If I have good experiences with a person, I expect more of the same. If I have bad experiences with a person, I also expect more of the same. For us, interaction consistency is more important than the result of the interaction itself. If I have labeled a person "bad" and this person behaves badly, my belief is reinforced. I have (in a way) a positive experience because my prior judgment was confirmed. I feel validated in my beliefs.

As humans, we value consistency very high. We value it highly in others, but first and foremost in our own experiences. We strive for *coherence* in our daily lives and feel good when our experiences and belief systems match.

Our basic psychological needs (control/orientation, enhancing self-worth, avoidance of pain, and attachment) play a significant role in this; control and orientation overlap greatly with consistency.[9]

We have different modes of assessment for our environment. Rational thought is only one of them — and maybe not even the most important one. Most of the information we get about our surroundings is analyzed unconsciously. This means that the subconscious very quickly sifts through all the incoming information rushing through our perception channels. It's a protection for the brain; if not, the brain would be completely overwhelmed.

The subconscious evaluates whether something is dangerous or threatening and also whether it's consistent with our prior experiences or not. Think about movies - when the villain tries to kill the hero; we are not surprised. We expect this much! We would be disappointed otherwise.

In our daily lives, we establish behavioral patterns in order to match our basic needs to our surroundings. These patterns first and foremost serve to keep us from harm. If something is good for us, if it's aligned to our basic needs, we tend to *seek more of it.*

If something is bad for us, we tend to try to *avoid* this experience. These avoidance patterns aim at not getting hurt (both physically and psychologically). They are designed to escape threats and disappointments. In a narrow scientific and psychological sense, that's motivation. Motivation means to be oriented towards something or to try to avoid it. When we fail to meet our motivational goals, we experience *incongruence.*[10]

Incongruence is unpleasant. We try our best to avoid it. Nevertheless, it's a fact of life that we have to go through it from time to time. Even more interesting than incongruence is *discordance.* Discordance happens when we are *torn* between avoiding something and seeking it.

That may sound strange at the beginning. But actually, most experiences are not black and white. They are not pleasant or unpleasant. More often than not, you must go through some degree of unpleasantness to reach your (ultimately pleasant) goal.

If you want to learn a new language, earn more money, or have a better life — all this will not come to you by magic. Whichever way you choose to pursue your goals, all options will require some degree of commitment and discipline. Many people like the idea of reaching a desired goal but not necessarily walking the stressful path towards it.

Unfortunately, this often leads to *stagnation* - the avoidance impulse and the seeking impulse block each other. In the end, nothing happens. It's an outstanding achievement and a step forward if you manage to get out of stagnation. It's great to embark on a journey, even if the outcome is unclear - especially *if* the outcome is unclear.

I said that the greatest task we have is to allow proximity without fusion and to accept vulnerability without lashing out for the sake of *self-protection.* This may not sound like much, but if you think about it, it's is a big thing! I'm absolutely convinced that many bad things we do are born from vulnerability.

Yes, we all do bad things. The more people are glued together, the more they can upset the other person. In psychology, this kind of being fused together is called a *symbiotic collective.* The term symbiosis is borrowed here from biology. In nature, symbiosis generally means that members of two different species work or live together in a win-win-situation - both species profit from it.

Whereas in biology, this is seen as positive, in psychology, the term has a negative connotation. Psychology-wise, symbiosis means that there is a certain form of dependence involved. Symbiosis is antagonistic when the inner development and autonomy of one partner are inhibited. In this case, we often see that symbiosis is bad for growth. Development is stalled when independence and gathering new information are *sacrificed* to fulfill basic needs like security and protection.

As humans, we want both.

We want to be *free*, and we need *attachment* - it is a life-long journey and a struggle to find a suitable balance between the two. In a symbiotic collective, two people behave complementarily. If we over-balance on the side of attachment, our personal development is inhibited. Taken together, we are as a couple fused into one personality.

Symbiotic is, therefore, every form of mutual behavior, which is characterized by insufficient boundaries. Disagreement is frowned upon. Conflict is taboo. Clear rules are avoided. Clear rules are avoided precisely because they entail the possibility of violation. If rules are violated, there will be conflict. And conflict is seen as bad in a symbiotic relationship.

Symbiotic relationships can be found everywhere. They can also take place in the classroom - I would even say that they can *especially* take place in the classroom. This is the case because two (or more) people have close contact with each other in class. If the teacher doesn't have a strong system of self-value and self-esteem, the danger that he or she will try to fill this void through the student is great.

Teacher-student-relationships are long-term in many cases. Depending on the subject, you can be stuck with a teacher (or a student for that matter) for years to come. There is a formal hierarchy (teacher-student), but also an informal one. Typically, the teacher is older, more experienced, and professionally more versed than the student.

In symbiotic relationships, the student's weaker position is used to boost the teacher's self-worth; I see this quite often. If nothing bad happens, this may even seem fair. But in case things go wrong, hell breaks loose. If the student fails an exam (for example), a fused teacher recognizes this not only as a professional mishap but also on a personal level as a *personal insult*.

This happens because the teacher's sense of self is a *reflected* one. In a reflected sense of self, how I feel about myself is greatly influenced by others. And how others (first and foremost, significant others) treat me and behave in general influences my well-being.

When I don't receive the positive reflected sense of self I crave, odds are I will lash out; I feel entitled to make clear that some unwritten rules have been violated. I may even feel obliged to do so. The inner rationalization machine will come up with some sort of justification (e.g., "I do it for your own good...").

I would say that the weaker your inner balance, the needier you are for outside validation and reflected self, and the more likely you are to mistreat others. Life is full of frustrations and difficult scenarios - that's simply a fact. This is how we grow. We *need* frustrations to grow. People who have a problem dealing with frustrations and easily take things as personal insults are prone to pushing others into *misery*.

More often than not, this is done in the name of *self-protection*. It's easier to rationalize bad behavior if it is seen as some level of protection against impending harm. Often it is overlooked (or rationalized away) that this act of "self-protection" brings a maximum of pain for the other person.[11]

Another frequently used rationalization strategy is to feign ignorance. "I had no idea this would hurt you; I hadn't thought you would take it like this; I was just joking." These sentences have in common that they seem to show a level of ignorance about the other person (and human interaction in general), which is hard to believe.

Attacking someone verbally needs a certain level of *insight* and *empathy* in the other person. In effect, the perfect aim required for an attack contradicts the backpedaling later. It's not credible to first attack someone very effectively and then act innocent, especially if it's evident that the attack was cleverly aimed and planned.

I believe that symbiotic relationships are much more common than we like to think. Remember, not all abuse is physical; whichever kind of abuse, it's very hard to undo the imprint of it (psychological or otherwise). It needs careful examination and processing by a trained professional to do so in a fair manner.

Depression and abuse have some things in common. Most prominent among them is that they tend to run through generations in families - they are "legacy issues."[12] They tend to be passed along from one generation to the other. Abuse and depression are closely linked. If you suffer from abuse, you are much more likely to develop depression.

I gladly take the danger of being called a "snowflake" when I say that we should not underestimate the harm done by psychological abuse. Un-nurturing relationships have a significant impact, especially during formative years of development (early childhood, puberty, early adulthood).

It is painful to address, but major causes of depression often stem from child abuse. This abuse can be physical, sexual or psychological, or even a mix of all three. This is why it is so important to look closely for signs of abuse when working with students.

From a therapy mindset, I believe that the process of recovery from depression needs a detailed analysis of past abusive experiences. Neuroscience shows that experiences we have change the chemistry, the architecture, and the responsiveness of the brain.

In the end, comparatively small dosages of stress lead to a full-blown stress reaction. The stress hormones released dock at multiple points in the brain. At these sites, they create havoc - sleep patterns are disturbed, nothing is fun anymore, everything seems senseless and tedious, and life is a chore. On top of that, the anxiety centers are stimulated.

Given the severity of the symptoms and level of suffering involved, it is clear that symbiotic relationships should be avoided at all costs. But that's easier said than done! On the receiving end, sometimes we have no choice but to enter or maintain a relationship even if we see it as abusive. We must do so in spite of the fact that we know that it's not good for us, for professional reasons, for example.

On the other end, it takes an awful lot of self-knowledge to avoid harming others in close relationships. We are both victims and perpetrators in one person. At different times we have different roles; therefore, I am convinced that we need deep self-examination to be good teachers.

If we want to avoid projection, avoid chaining others to us in symbiotic relationships, and avoid engaging in abusive behavior, we need a strongly developed sense of self. It needs a willingness to accept uncomfortable truths about ourselves. It also needs to be willing to go along the hard path of personal growth. In short, it needs "meaningful endurance" (Schnarch).[13]

Important points to remember

✓ We need a scientific approach to education and learning. Brain activation only correlates to mental activity.

✓ The tools we have at our disposal in a situation determine whether we feel stress or not: Cognition is involved in leading to an appraisal.

✓ Everyday emotional abuse leaves no trace. There is no physical evidence, and yet it can be immensely harmful to the individual. We are victims and perpetrators in one person. At different times we have different roles.

✓ Symbiosis is antagonistic when the inner development and autonomy of one partner are inhibited. As humans, we want to be free, and we need attachment.

✓ In symbiotic relationships, the sense of self is a reflected one - how I feel about myself is greatly influenced by others.

✓ Abuse and depression are closely linked. If you suffer from abuse, you are much more likely to develop depression.

Chapter references

1   Lazarus, Richard S (2000): "Toward Better Research on Stress and Coping." *American Psychologist*, Vol. 55. No. 6, 665 673.

2   See for more information: Smith, Craig A., & Kirby, Leslie D. (2009): "Putting appraisal in context: Toward a relational model of appraisal and emotion." *Cognition and Emotion*, 23 (7), 1352–1372.

3   An idea found in many works of philosophy, e.g., Nietzsche's "Genealogy of Morals."

4   I refer here to Jung, C.G. (1996): *The Archetypes and the Collective Unconscious*. London. Routledge.

5   See Verduyn, P., van Mechelen, I., & Tuerlinckx, F. (2011): "The relation between event processing and the duration of emotional experience." *Emotion*, 11, 20–28.

6   This term most probably stems from Jung. For more information, see Segal, Robert A. (1999): *Theorizing about myth*. Amherst: University of Massachusetts Press.

7   See for more information, Mantel, Gerhard (2003): *Mut zum Lampenfieber. Mentale Strategien für Musiker zur Bewältigung von Auftritts- und Prüfungsangst*. Mainz: Serie Musik Atlantis, Schott.

8   See: Schnarch (2011, 211).

9   Seymour Epstein formulated the Cognitive-experiential self-theory (CEST) as a dual-process model of perception. He strongly proposed control and orientation as a guiding principle. He also said that all these basic needs are equal in their relative importance. If even one of them is unfulfilled over a longer period of time, the personality structure may crumble.

10   More information you find in Grawe's excellent book "Neuropsychotherapy."

11   You can see this also very clearly in politics.

12   An excellent article on this topic can be found here: https://www.psychologytoday.com/us/articles/200305/child-abuse-and-depression

13   Schnarch, David (2011): *Intimacy and Desire*. New York: Beaufort books.

Chapter 13

Stretching the Comfort Zone: Self-development and Mindfulness

We need a strongly developed sense of self. We need it in life in general, but we especially need it when teaching others. If we fail to work on a stable sense of who we are and who we want to be, we are in danger of *projecting* our own deficiencies on others. Projection is very powerful.

Projection often happens entirely on a subconscious level; it's a defense mechanism that helps us avoid facing some aspects of ourselves. We are not perfect people - we have good and bad sides. While this is a truism, it's actually very hard (and rare) to face difficult aspects.

Here is where projection comes into play. Projection means that you attribute to others your own dark sides to better cope with them.[1] I can plausibly deny myself of having a destructive impulse if I attribute it to others instead. Quite often, we try to heal ourselves on the backs of other people. If I shift and project my bad feelings on someone else, I can pour all my disdain, anger, and negative emotions on that person.

I don't have to deal with them myself. I don't have to face the reality of myself with these issues; instead, I can elevate myself above the other person and act out my subconscious impulses. This may feel great short-term, but it will not solve the underlying problems long-term.

A very typical example is a person bullying other people. This is mostly born from a deep sense of vulnerability projected on others and then subsequently addressed with aggressiveness. By tormenting the other person, the bully seeks to mitigate their inner sense of lacking self-worth and vulnerability.

The blame is often administered to the victim, "You deserve being treated badly because you are weak." In addition to being poorly treated, the victim is shamed on top of that. It's a blame game, a toxic process.

Teachers must think critically about how they speak. A lot of psychological "hygiene" is needed. Projection comes easy but is hard to remedy. If you do not work on your communication style, the danger is great that you unconsciously project your own anxieties and lacking self-worth on others.[2]

If you do not work on your communication style, the danger is great that you unconsciously project your own anxieties and lacking self-worth on others.

We all suffer from anxiety — it's a fact of our existence. Also, we all suffer from lacking self-worth. It's difficult to address; most people don't like to talk or even think about it. It's not a topic for polite chitchat. If you are like most people, then you have these issues as well. I certainly do. If people look closely into their hearts, they see that they perceive themselves as somewhat *lacking*.

It's this feeling of not being enough, not fulfilling one's full promise, of being somewhat *wrong*. We tend to think that this deficiency will go away if we climb just one more mountain, earn a little bit more money, or reach the next rung on the social ladder. But it doesn't work that way.

Whenever you reach a certain goal, there is already something else on the horizon, urging you to go on in this direction. It's like in Kafka's story "Before the Law," where the door opens just to reveal an unending row of further doors to be opened. [3]

If we are not aware of our feeling of being lacking, we are tempted to project it on others. The first step out of this dynamic is to become aware of this feeling - accomplishing that in and of itself is no small feat! Many teachers I meet professionally deny having deficiencies there. They say, "Everything's fine with me; it's others who have a problem." But when you dig a little deeper, you see that's not entirely true.

To be precise, *truth* is not a valuable way of thinking about these matters at all. Come to think about it, it's clear that it *doesn't matter* who is right or who is wrong. At the end of the day, the only person you can directly influence at any given situation you find yourself in is *yourself*. So, even if the other person might be wrong, you cannot directly change him or her.

You can only change *your own behavior*. Because we act in social systems, changes within the system will affect further change. By doing something about yourself, you affect change in the other person. This might seem outlandish in the beginning, but it's the *only way*. Your changed behavior will force the other person to accommodate to it and change conversely.

You can try to coerce or manipulate other people, and in the short run, this will give you results very fast. But in the long run, odds are that people will switch back to their former behavior when you stop putting pressure on them - the psychology of learning tells us that much.

If we want to avoid projection, avoid chaining others to us in symbiotic relationships, and avoid engaging in abusive behavior, we need a strongly developed sense of *self*. This needs a willingness to accept uncomfortable truths about ourselves. It also needs to be willing to go along the hard path of personal growth and needs "meaningful endurance" (Schnarch).[4]

There is a sub-branch of psychology devoted to how we read other people and how we can positively affect change in others through our own behavior. It's called mentalization (although it has other names as well. Schnarch calls it "mind-mapping."). It's a fascinating topic — I'm certain that we need a strong basis of empathy and self-knowledge to use mentalization in a good way.

This brings me to the art of looking deeply into yourself (*introspection* in scientific terms). Introspection means that you try to get to know yourself better, to understand your habits and patterns, and by doing so, you can avoid the pitfalls of blindly charging into something. It offers you the opportunity to understand what triggers you.

We all have triggers. We all have specific painful experiences or perceived deficiencies, which we try hard to keep others from seeing; it's perfectly normal. As they say, ignorance is bliss. That might be true, but ignorance about yourself tempts you to follow old patterns, which can be harmful to you and others.

Self-knowledge and self-development are worthy goals. There are quite a lot of methods you can use to get there - one is *therapy*. When you train to become a therapist, you must undergo therapy yourself. I think that's a very valuable experience, and I would go so far as to say that teachers should undergo a short therapy experience themselves. I'm sure this would help to avoid many problems further down the road.

Apart from therapy, *meditation* is a very useful tool for gaining self-knowledge. I meditate every day. Nowadays, there is a lot of information out there, apps you can use, and instructional videos you can watch. I urge you to do exactly that. Even if you decide that meditation is not for you, I guarantee that you will benefit from learning about it. (If only to have an informed opinion.)

Over the years, I tried several approaches to meditation - there are many. I would like to encourage you to try a few and see what works for you and what doesn't. Meditation practice seems suspect to some people (although this changes at the moment) because it comes with many associations.

There are a variety of different paths to choose from. In recent years, some brilliant scientists and scholars worked very hard to offer meditation techniques to westerners. These approaches are uncluttered from excess religious baggage, which is very positive. First and foremost, among them are Jon Kabat-Zinn and MBSR.

Looking deeply into yourself can be done within any framework - the important thing is to really do it. Meditation does not require us to leave behind our rationality. I'm sure that we can boost our well-being without throwing overboard valuable knowledge we already have. In the end, it is about learning something about ourselves, nothing more.

When you start, I very much recommend breathing exercises combined with walking meditation. In my own experience, walking meditation is wonderful! I had big trouble concentrating on my breathing in the beginning. Walking meditation made things much easier and opened up this whole realm for me.

In walking meditation, you walk slowly, trying to match the rhythm of your steps with your breathing. Try to be aware of how your feet touch the floor, how your weight is aligned on your feet, and look deeply into it. There are many things you can focus on once you start paying attention to how you walk![5]

Looking deeply is a term I really like. You can also use the name *mindfulness*.[6] Mindfulness is excellent; it is everywhere and often paired with talk about resilience. Resilience is the ability to withstand negative influences and adapt to challenging surroundings. That's a great feature! Ultimately, meditation will build your resilience, but we must be aware of these practices being instrumentalized. It's utterly wrong to force people to accept dire circumstances in the name of resilience.

"Just be more resilient!" is not a valuable help in trying situations. (Actually, that's a kind of shame dumping). Imagine a challenging situation at work; your boss is mean to you. It's very easy for the boss to turn around and say, "Be more resilient!" instead of addressing his or her own behavior. Growth and development always start with oneself — and that's also true for the boss.

What mindfulness means is being open to what's going on in your mind at that moment. Therefore, mindfulness teachings are often *deceptively simple*; you will learn very fast that, in truth, they are not simple at all! In mindfulness meditation, you are asked to acknowledge what's going on in your mind and not judge it.

That's already heavy stuff! We are so prone to constantly judging ourselves and our surroundings that it's deeply engrained. Our whole society works that way. There are always winners and losers; losers are bad, and the winner takes all. Performance matters; competition is everywhere.

I'm very critical of this. Competition has its upsides, but it also generates a lot of misery. We are always forced to perform and fight. Out of this, a lot of stress and anxiety are generated. As a teacher, I often encounter the paradox that students are unable to reach their full potential simply out of fear. They do not fail because something is lacking, they don't work hard enough, or aren't talented enough. They fail precisely because they fear *failing*.

We worry; it's part of being human, but it can also be a disorder. Approximately one in five people in the US suffer from anxiety, and these numbers are rising. It might be because we look more closely at these matters nowadays, but personally, I believe it has a lot to do with scarce resources, competition, and judgment by others.

The fear of failing is a trained behavior. Young children (generally) don't have it. They explore. Coming of age, self-consciousness settles in, and with self-consciousness, difficult questions tend to arise. Who am I? How do others see me? Do I belong? Am I loved?

These questions all imply judgment — by others, but also by myself. If I base my self-worth on how others see me, I'm in for a lot of pain. I learn to accept the judgement of others as true. I am trained to fear others' judgment because they can damage me and my self-worth, and I will try to avoid that since avoidance of pain is a basic psychological need.

Avoidance tends to multiply our misery; it spirals out of control. On top of a bad situation, we now have to deal with being fearful of our fears. It goes on and on. Neuroscientist Joseph LeDoux recently argued that avoidance is not always bad.[7] But the principle still holds; avoidance tends to be harmful.

In therapy, *exposure* is used to work around avoidance. Exposure means that you confront the issue, which makes you anxious. In a controlled setting, you experience and have contact with what gives you fear. The important point is that you encounter the anxiety source *without danger.* This allows reducing the fear response.

Since the only thing the brain can't do, is not to learn, the brain learns that the fear response is unnecessary. Doing so helps to overcome feelings of distress and anxiety. This works very well, and there is a ton of empirical evidence to its effectiveness.[8]

The exposure technique is a combination of confrontation and relaxation. We are unable to be relaxed and afraid at the same time - it's mutually exclusive. If you think about nature, this becomes obvious. Our fear response is evolutionally "designed" to help us cope with difficult situations. It offers us a set of responses (fight, flight, freeze), which we then use to get somehow out of the clinch.

Our stress responses in the body are meant to activate us, to allow us to run faster, see more sharply, and hear more acutely. This reaction is modulated by the sympathetic nervous system; all its efforts go contrary to relaxation.

In relaxation, the *para*sympathetic system is activated. Both systems work complementary against each other like a rocker:[9] They are antagonists. When we are relaxed, when we rest, the body is not ready for fighting. Instead, it is in "rest-and-digest" or "feed and breed" mode.

These two systems (parasympathetic system and sympathetic system) are complementary, which means they can't be activated both simultaneously. And that's already the key here. We can counter our stress response if we learn a relaxation technique because the systems involved are *mutually exclusive.*

In exposure therapy, the therapist identifies what makes the patient anxious. Then the therapist practices a relaxation technique with the patient. When this is accomplished, they try to confront the situation that is giving the patient fear. They do that in small steps, beginning at a very low level of anxiety.

Imagine you are afraid to speak in public. If I tell you, "Imagine you are in a fully-packed stadium, everybody is looking at you, and now you have to give a speech on which rests the future of the world," this will give you the creeps. (Actually, it did give me the creeps just writing this down now.)

With a low-level situation, "Imagine speaking to a friend in a bar," you might be much more comfortable with. Then we can gradually use stronger situations like, "Imagine speaking at a family function" or "Imagine raising your voice at a team meeting." It is a series of steps, one step building on the other in strength and challenge.

By going through the process step-by-little-step in a calm and relaxed setting, you will discover that you can bear these situations. It is critical to learn to become relaxed first.

There are different approaches. One is to do this in real life (*in vivo* is the fancy Latin term). In the example of being afraid of public speaking, this means going out there and (yes) speaking publicly in a controlled setting.

That's already tough stuff. Actually, I recommend that only as a second step. I prefer starting with doing things in imagination (*in sensu*). The mind has this wonderful capability of being able to imagine things deeply. At a certain point, it is even hard to distinguish between reality and imagination. Many visualization techniques use this process where real world and imaginative approaches can be easily combined.[10]

With my own clients and students, I like to start with imagination first. Remember that this only works after a relaxed state is established. Relaxation is so important! Most of the time, we are not relaxed at all. When you start working with others on their relaxation, you will most likely understand just how stressed people are even under *normal* circumstances.

The same holds true for yourself. I was amazed when I first went through deep relaxation. I realized how many (minor) stressors I was accustomed to constantly overlooking! I couldn't believe how stressed I was without really knowing it. A few years back, I went to the dentist, and he told me that I would need a bite-guard. He could see that I was crunching my teeth so badly at night that I needed a dental splint for sleeping.

This was, of course, due to stress. The interesting thing is that I had no idea how bad my stress level really was. Many people have experiences like this. We are working very hard. We push ourselves a lot. And we are stressed without realizing it.

Here, meditation enters the picture. From a therapy point of view, meditation shares a lot of properties with exposure therapy. In meditation, we try to relax through breathing exercises. Then we attempt to look at the content of our consciousness without judgment. In a later step, we can expose ourselves during meditation to thoughts and fears we have and which we tend to avoid in everyday life.

Because it is a learning experience, it will change your brain. The gray matter will become denser in areas of the brain important for memory, regulating emotions, and self-awareness. If we manage to reach a state of looking at our inner workings with a calm mind, we have already won! The quality of inner calm has the power to mitigate pain, reduce anxiety, and make our brain work better.

Believe me, although it sounds easy, that's super hard. My biggest problem with meditation (and MBSR) is that it's so simple to describe what you have to do — and, in effect, immensely hard to do it. Just sitting on a cushion and focusing on your breath doesn't sound like much, right? Let me be honest; the sitting part is easy!

But once you sit for some time, thoughts will pop up. You will start to think, ruminate, and remember. Thoughts will come to the surface, which is not easy to handle - some you may wish to avoid. It will soon become clear to you that meditation is an intense experience of self, a confrontation with everything you are made of. That can be quite excruciating.

I went to a "day of mindfulness" where a few participants had to leave the hall early; sitting in silence was too much to bear for them. I can understand that. Sometimes I feel like getting up and leaving. I'm writing about these difficulties because I think that sometimes they get swept under the rug. Still, I would like to recommend to you to go and meditate.

I believe mastering meditation requires a lot of discipline and (maybe) some special talent. The good news is that you don't have to become a master! The benefits will show very fast, without having to become a monk in the Himalayas.

When you start to meditate, you will discover just how distracted you are nearly all the time - and that's a great victory! As the meditation masters say, "When you know that you are distracted, you have taken the first (and most important) step." I have huge problems with being judgmental towards myself. The mistake I frequently make when meditating is to berate myself for being distracted.

Being distracted is absolutely normal! We tend to day-dream or follow our anxieties into inner monologues of fear and anger like Alice follows the rabbit down the rabbit hole in "Alice in Wonderland." If we become aware of our distractions and maybe — just maybe — we manage for a few short moments to free ourselves from these distractions, then we have accomplished a lot.

Very rarely have I experienced feeling truly calm inside during meditation. These experiences are few, but I can tell you that these moments are worth it. Even if you can't easily replicate them again, the memory stays with you. And it is this memory, which will change your view on what you experience in your day-to-day lives.

For example, I realized just how much I was caught in a constant inner dialogue. I also realized how much I was used to avoiding unpleasant situations and staying with pleasant sensations. That's completely human, of course.

But in reality, what pushes us forward towards personal growth are mostly unpleasant experiences - they force us to regroup and reconsider ourselves. (That's what Schnarch is saying by using the term meaningful endurance.) In my life, I learned that most of the challenges I had to go through were during times when everything was not smooth sailing.

If you want to start, there are many meditation instructions available online - I strongly recommend trying it out. I've already talked about the "mindfulness-based stress reduction" (MBSR) program by Jon Kabat-Zinn, which is now taught in schools, hospitals, universities, and (it feels like) almost everywhere. For beginners, it's best to start with guided meditations.

Meditation is a means to notice our subjectivity and maybe develop a new strength - the power to establish some distance between our ideas about reality and reality itself. In my opinion, it's already a miracle when we understand (genuinely understand) that the stories we tell ourselves about reality are not the truth.

We must develop a healthy distance towards our own judgments. The danger I see is that we project our own value judgments on the students. Unfortunately, our educational system (as our society in general) values assimilation and conformity very highly. I often see that it's difficult for students to talk about things, which do not conform to our society's values. If students learn to simply accept our value judgments as true, they fail at developing their own structures.

Therefore, I would like to refer you to university meditation programs, which are available free of charge online (Harvard and UCLA, for example).[11] If you like to learn more about it, I recommend reading the books by Jon Kabat-Zinn.[12] As in most things, training regularly is the key to success.[13]

If mindfulness means becoming aware of what's happening now, then starting with what you're doing *anyway* is a good start. At least, I think so. In the beginning, I couldn't believe that just being aware of what's happening right now could feel good, but it's true.

Personal growth doesn't come easy. Many relationships we are in (at work, at home, everywhere) are challenging. They challenge us and our sense of complacency. Whether you grow or not makes the difference between learning something positive from a challenge or admitting defeat.

If you have no positive take-aways, the challenge was just an ordeal. If you actually learn something, the difficult situation may have been beneficial for you in the long run. If you are willing and able to endure pain for the sake of growth, then you can work towards meaningful change.

As humans, we tend to clutch onto things to feel safe - to be open to change has a lot to do with personal integrity. Integrity is something internal, making you feel consistent inside. I'm always amazed when I see people willing to throw their integrity overboard for meager gains (financial, career, or otherwise). When you violate principles you hold dear, you will feel dreadful afterward. The experience will diminish and dishonor you, and you might feel shame.

I hate to bring it to you, but it's true. Ultimately, the only security you can find is the relationship with yourself. In order to see this security, you must develop a strong inner balance. This balance allows you then to be solid inside and also flexible in your responses. It helps you to stay calm and endure adversity.[14] And it enables you to respond appropriately.

In law, this is called the principle of *proportionality* - your actions should correspond to what the other person has said or done. I believe that some sort of mental hygiene is necessary to accomplish this. Maybe long walks work for you, or perhaps you can unwind working out. The path I propose is to look deeply into yourself using some sort of meditation approach. If you can develop a strong inner balance, your students will benefit immensely.

Important points to remember

✓   Teachers need psychological "hygiene." Projection comes easy but is hard to remedy.

✓   The only person you can directly influence in any given situation is yourself. We act in social systems, and changes within the system will affect further change in others.

✓   Apart from therapy, meditation is a very useful tool for gaining self-knowledge and doing psychological hygiene. Meditation can be entirely non-religious.

✓   Resilience is the ability to withstand negative influences and adapt to challenging surroundings.

✓   Avoidance tends to multiply our misery. Exposure means that you confront the issue, which makes you anxious in a controlled setting.

✓   We need a strongly developed sense of self to navigate relationships successfully.

Chapter references

1   Malancharuvil, JM (2004): "Projection, introjection, and projective identification: a reformulation" *American Journal of Psychoanalysis*, 64 (4): 375–82.

2   See Mantel (2003, 67-68).

3   Kafka, Franz (1995): *The Complete Stories*. New York: Schocken; Reprint Edition

4   Schnarch, David (2011): *Intimacy and Desire*. New York: Beaufort books.

5   You find a guide to walking meditation here: https://www.lionsroar.com/how-to-meditate-thich-nhat-hanh-on-walking-meditation/

6   As one example among a multitude, here is the current Amazon No.1 bestseller on mindfulness: Sockolov, Matthew (2018): *Practicing Mindfulness: 75 Essential Meditations to Reduce Stress, Improve Mental Health, and Find Peace in the Everyday*. Emeryville: Althea Press.

7   https://opinionator.blogs.nytimes.com/2013/04/07/for-the-anxious-avoidance-can-have-an-upside/

8   As one among many: Böhnlein, Joscha; Altegoer, Luisa; Muck, Nina Kristin; Roesmann, Kati; Redlich, Ronny; Dannlowski, Udo; Leehr, Elisabeth J. (2020): "Factors influencing the success of exposure therapy for specific phobia: A systematic review". In: *Neuroscience & Biobehavioral Reviews*, 108: 796–820.

9   See for more information: McCorry, LK (2007): "Physiology of the autonomic nervous system". In: *American Journal of Pharmaceutical Education*, 71 (4): 78.

10   For more information, see Hezel, Dianne M.; Simpson, H. Blair (2019): "Exposure and response prevention for obsessive-compulsive disorder: A review and new directions." *Indian Journal of Psychiatry*, 61 (Suppl 1): S85–S92.
Abramowitz, Jonathan S.; Deacon, Brett J.; Whiteside, Stephen P. H. (2011): *Exposure Therapy for Anxiety: Principles and Practice*. New York: Guilford Press.

11   Here are links to free of charge online meditations from UCLA and Harvard:
https://www.uclahealth.org/marc/mindful-meditations
https://davidvago.bwh.harvard.edu/how-to-meditate-links-for-guided-meditation-practice/|

12   Kabat-Zinn, Jon (2005): Wherever You Go, There You Are. New York: Hachette Books.

13   Actually, formal sitting meditation is only one possibility you have, albeit a very powerful one. I already told you about walking meditation, which works great for me. Another option is the use of gathas. Gathas are very short poems (only a few lines). You can tell them to yourself while doing ordinary things: Eating, washing up, walking, even brushing your teeth. Gathas have a long history of meditation practice. I cam by them through the Zen master Thich Nhat Hanh. If you're interested, you can find some gathas here:
https://www.stillwatermpc.org/practice-resources/mindfulness-gathas/

14   More on this in Schnarch (2009).

Chapter 14

"The Inner Yoga Mat"
or Inner Balance and Mentalization

It's clear how vital a strong inner balance is - life is no easy ride. Whatever you do, wherever you live, you will have to deal with challenging situations. You will have to face adversity sooner or later.

An inner balance allows you to measure your responses. Actually, this is a question that has been on my mind for a long time. How do we know how to behave in a particular situation? How do we *know* what other people might think about us? Or what they don't think? How do we get through even a single day without getting into screaming matches and fist-fights all the time?

These questions are fundamental as a teacher. We interact with people all the time. We must read them, form an idea of what's going on in their minds, and guess at their motivations. All this is difficult — and also easy to misunderstand. We never really know what's going on with other people, but we might make reasonable guesses.

This has greatly to do with being socialized into a given group, learning how to behave in a society, and being raised in (some sort of) a family. Scientists call that *enculturation.*[1]

Enculturation is a process, and by going through it, we learn how the culture around us works. We learn which rules apply and when they apply. We obtain norms and values and get to know worldviews. This whole and lengthy process is shaped by the people we interact with. It goes on through our whole life (with influences from parents, friends, co-workers, etc.).

As a father, I can tell you that it's a long process to make your kid compatible with the world around you! The goal of this process of enculturation is *competence* - to be competent in interacting with others of the same culture and to know precisely when to apply which rules. (Acting in different cultures simultaneously is an even more complicated matter altogether!)

After gaining this knowledge, we are able to adapt and change our behavior very quickly. Desmond Morris gives a powerful example of this fact. A London actress might be perfectly comfortable with eccentric, even outrageous behavior on stage (if required by the play performed). Still, the same actress would — say, meeting the queen at a charity show — "fall back immediately upon medieval manners and dip her body in an ancient curtsey."[2]

We get from others the knowledge about norms and their application by forming a general background knowledge. Norms, values, and general background knowledge are one thing. The other (in my opinion, even more important) ingredient is the *mental faculties necessary* to use them. Norms are useless if you don't have a mind capable of discerning how to read a given situation. We need to read other people to get into meaningful exchanges with them.

We've already seen that our mind doesn't manipulate reality directly - direct influence is impossible. Instead, we work with *representations*. We see something, and then we form a mental image from it. To do so, we use the experiences and memories we already have. For example, do you remember the first time you've seen an optical illusion?

Optical illusions are cool. They seem to show two conflicting images at the same time. In truth, it's clear that the objective reality does not change; the drawing on the paper stays the same. But our perception of it shifts. In fancy talk, optical illusions are therefore called *multi-stable stimuli*. The brain (not being sure which possible interpretation is correct) presents both available options to the conscious mind - it shifts between them.[3]

The visual system comes to wrong conclusions; it's actually very easy for this to occur. The visual system doesn't deliver a mirror image of reality. Rather, it interprets the electric impulses reaching the brain through our sensory channels and reconstructs a representation.

Now comes the clincher - when you see the same optical illusion again after some time, it lost much of its confusing quality. Your brain already learned to accept it. So, the way we perceive the world is shaped on a mental level by the brain capabilities we have and the experiences we've gone through. (Here, enculturation comes into play).

Optical illusions are an easy example - much more complicated is how we see and interpret other people. Actually, *interpretation* is the key term here. We never know precisely what others feel or think. We can talk with them, but there is no guarantee at all that they will tell us what's going on in their minds. Maybe they don't even know what's going on in there!

It's always an act of attribution when we say, "Someone feels such and such." We interpret other people frequently. We get clues from their behavior, their tone of voice, the words they use, the way they dress — you name it. Then we take this knowledge and subconsciously interpret what these people might feel, what they might think, and what their intentions might be.

Ekman did a lot of research on this topic.[4] With all due caution, we can say that at least basic types of internal states can be attributed to others. This can be done reliably. Interestingly, all cultures world-wide seem to share these expressions.

On an even more fundamental level, this type of attribution rests on recognizing others as *similar to us*. Only when we understand that other people act and feel like we do can we attempt to understand their behavior.[5] This is by no means a given. I remember (when I was a student) that there was a widespread prejudice among westerners against Asian people (the idea being that "they don't feel emotions the same way we do," especially nervousness, anxiety, and stress).[6]

Ekman recorded the facial expressions of different people from around the globe when experiencing some standard situations. He found that a limited set of facial expressions is shared among people worldwide. He called this set "basic emotions." (If they are real emotions is a long discussion.)

His findings show that even if we cannot speak with each other because we have no common language, we share a nonverbal vocabulary to convey some essential bits of information. In some basic situations, we can communicate effectively without words, no matter where people are from.

The standard expressions Ekman found include happiness, grief, sadness, surprise, or being repulsed. These are communicated through tiny changes in our smiles, the way our eyes are tilted, if we crease our brow, etc. We use mimic signs, so to speak, which are understood everywhere.

We don't know exactly how this works. One theory is that we simulate other people's feelings within ourselves. By doing so, we get an understanding of what the other person might feel. We do so based on our own emotions.

This makes a lot of sense to me.

If we put ourselves in someone else's shoes, we can attribute our own feelings to this person. We still don't know what precisely the *other person feels*, but we get an inkling of how *we* might feel in the given situation. This is a conclusion and an interpretation of clues; it's not what the other person really feels.

As humans, we can feel with and for others - that we have this amazing ability never fails to surprise me. Even if we know intellectually that the shown emotions are *fake*, we can be moved to tears. When we see a movie, for example, our mind's rational side knows precisely that these are highly trained, paid professionals interacting with each other. Still, the performance can sweep us off our feet.

Why does this work? Neuroscience has done a lot of research into this. Throughout the brain, there are many areas with the ability to "mirror" other people's behavior. Neurons specialized to do so are accordingly called *mirror neurons.*

Neuron fires

Neuron fires

Monkey does action   Monkey sees action

Mirror neurons react regardless of whether I do something or I observe someone else doing it.

Mirror neurons react regardless of whether I do something or someone else does. Our individual experiences are the foundation for this - I match someone else based on what I know and what I've already experienced. So, my *own* motor repertoire is the tool kit at my disposal. Unfortunately, this sets limits; otherwise, I could learn how to play like a great artist simply by watching him or her.

Mirror neurons are crucial to learning. They make it easier for us to imitate a movement and play a role in developing empathy towards others. The argument here is that by mirroring someone else's pain, for example, we kind of feel it ourselves. Therefore, we get a representation of the other's pain. Since avoidance of pain is a basic psychological need of humans, we tend to try to ease the other's suffering.

Mirror neurons are very active when we interact with other people. A prime example of this is music-making. Actively making music engages brain regions "that largely overlap with the human MNS" (mirror neuron system).[7] It seems that many different parts of the brain have areas with mirror abilities.[8] You can be sure they are there for a reason.

Learning is a social strategy; we need others to learn from. We also need to be able to *understand* what they are doing. We must understand what they're showing us to really grasp what's going on. We need to work together for this to be successful. And we need to understand how others manipulate their surroundings for the desired result. We must reliably be able to attribute intentions to their behavior - you may call that *cognitive empathy*.

As science goes, thinking about learning and interaction like this is a relatively recent thing (the last twenty years or so). Before, scientists largely focused on how *one person* acts, speaks, and does something. A seismic shift occurred when it became clear that you need someone else to understand you in order to talk successfully. (It seems terribly apparent in retrospect, but what a great revelation at that time!)

Something similar happened in psychology. Psychologists understood that (in our minds) we never directly interact with the outside world. Our brain is locked into a skull without any means of directly influencing the outside world. We continuously try to make sense of our surroundings. The brain's main job is to draw conclusions from what we already know and then to make reasonable guesses about what might happen in the near future - all this to keep us from harm.

The mind always tries to make reasonable guesses. It has the ability to be aware of *itself* - that's pretty amazing! Psychologists established the term mentalization for that. Mentalization means that I can be aware of what I feel. Also, I can influence what I feel through this knowledge. We can regulate our *affects* (as the psychologists say).[9]

Most times, we are not aware that we mentalize. But actually, it is something we need to learn. Newborn babies do not have this ability yet. Mentalization means understanding yourself and others' behavior related to internal states. These internal mental states can be all sorts of feelings, needs, and reasons.

When we attribute intentions to others, we mentalize without knowing it. Many mental processes are totally below the level of consciousness. Simply because we are not consciously aware of something doesn't mean it's not going on. This makes absolute sense because scarce conscious resources are freed for more important matters.

When you speak with other people, you mentalize. You don't know it, but your brain constantly evaluates other people and attributes mental states to them. This way, we adjust quickly when the mood in a discussion changes. It might be hard to pinpoint exactly what happened, and you might not even know. But your brain adjusts quickly if there is a different feeling to a situation.

Conscious mentalization comes in handy when there is conflict. It allows us to try to understand what's going on within ourselves and the other person. It's putting yourself in someone else's shoes. It's the attempt to see past behavior and to detect *intentions*. Very quickly, we simulate how we would feel or react in a given situation, so we can then talk with the other person about it.

Mentalization is a way to try to make sense of misunderstandings - putting yourself in the other's shoes is simulating the other's mind within your mind. "What would I do?" or "What is she feeling?" By asking these questions, you have both simultaneously your and the other person's mind inside your mind your mind.[10]

By simulating the other's mind, you get a sense of what he or she might feel. This allows you to develop empathy. Empathy, in turn, is the basis of self-regulation. Personally, I think that *emotional self-regulation* is immensely important in teaching. As I see it, we continuously need to acknowledge how we feel ourselves. And we need to develop a reasonably reliable estimate of how the other person *might* feel.

As I said, the only security you can find in interactions is the *relationship with yourself*. To mentalize under stress, you must develop a strong inner balance. This balance lets you be firm inside and at the same time elastic in your responses - it helps you to stay grounded. And it allows you to respond *appropriately* under different conditions.

The principle of proportionality states that your actions should match what the other person has said or done. If this is put into effect, escalation should not occur. We know that in real life, that's not the case. Discussions tend to get out of hand; things escalate, and we hold grudges. All this is perfectly normal (but not very desirable).

We need to identify what triggers us; we need *trigger analysis*. Every person has issues. Every person has vulnerabilities. Every person has some neuralgic points. (I certainly have them!) If you push there, the person will jump. Experiences we had before come into play here; they prime us to behave in a certain manner.

If we perceive a situation as dangerous, our alarm system is triggered. When we experience the same or a similar situation, the alarm will go off again and more manageable this time. We are already on guard, expecting mischief. Thus trigger analysis makes us assess which triggers we have. It can also be used to understand what triggers another person.

I always like to say that "teaching is a joint venture." It's something we do together. Like many other activities, it's impossible to do it alone. There is always a recipient of your teaching (even if this person exists only in your imagination). Therefore, we need to be very conscious of ourselves and the other person.

We need to understand ourselves better and develop inner strength. This enables us then to choose our reactions in difficult situations. If we don't have enough inner strength, our *temper* will decide for us, and we will give in to impulses. I'm convinced that a lot of misery can be avoided if we learn how to cope better with (negative or challenging) emotions.

Zen master, Thich Nhat Hanh, said that the amount of suffering in the world is enormous.[11] This makes the work of teaching very difficult. As teachers, we have a great privilege - we can actively try to make a difference. I'm certain that this difference starts with the way we interact with each other and how we talk with each other.[12]

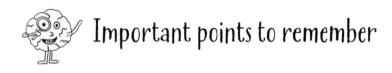# Important points to remember

✓   The goal of enculturation is competence.

✓   The way we perceive the world is shaped on a mental level by the brain capabilities we have and the experiences we've gone through.

✓   Throughout the brain, there are many areas with the ability to "mirror" other people's behavior. Neurons specialized to do so are called mirror neurons.

✓   Mentalization means that I can be aware of what I feel. We can regulate our *affects*. When we attribute intentions to others, we mentalize without knowing it.

✓   By simulating the other's mind, we get a sense of what he or she might feel. This allows you to develop empathy.

✓   Empathy, in turn, is the basis of self-regulation. Self-regulation is important for putting distance to our habitual impulses.

Chapter references

1   See for details: Grusec, Joan E.; Hastings, Paul D (2007): *Handbook of Socialization: Theory and Research*. New York: Guilford Press; p 547.

2   This quote is found on page 19 of Morris, Desmond (2002): *Peoplewatching: The Desmond Morris Guide to Body Language*. New York: Vintage

3   More on this in Eagleman, David (2012): Incognito. Edinburgh: Canongate Books

4   Ekman has been controversial. There is some critique of his methodologies. As I understand it, he still falls into the "mind-body-trap." His research (at best) shows that there is global coherence on how certain mental states are communicated non-verbally. No further conclusions on the nature of these emotions are valid from my point of view. Although momentous for the theory of cultural understanding, Ekman's findings do not offer insights into the inherent nature of emotion. Rather, his research has shown that a semiotic system exists to communicate emotions through facial expressions. More detailed information can be found in Ekman's book (2003): *Emotions Revealed. Recognizing Faces and Feelings to Improve Communication and Emotional Life*. New York: Times Books (Henry Holt and Company).

5   See for more information: Tomasello, Michael (2006): *Die kulturelle Entwicklung des menschlichen Denkens. Zur Evolution der Kognition*. [Nachdruck]. Frankfurt am Main: Suhrkamp.

6   This was, of course, because of great performances by Asian musicians. Obviously, this is racist (even if maybe without intent).

7   See Wan et al. (2010, 161).

8   Mukamel et al. (2010, 750) conclude: "multiple systems in humans may be endowed with neural mechanisms of mirroring both the integration and differentiation of perceptual and motor aspects of actions performed by the self and others."

9   Allen/Fonagy (see 2006, xvi) describes this ability as most relevant for the formation of interpersonal relationships.

10   For more information, see Hagelquist, J.Ø (2015): *The Mentalization Guidebook*. London: Karnac Books.

11 See Weare, Katherine, Hanh, Thich Nhat (2017): *Happy teachers change the world. A guide for cultivating mindfulness in education.* Berkeley: Parallax Press.

12 This is also the basic idea of Rosenberg's non-violent communication (NVC).

PART 3

Teaching is something we do together; it involves communication. Actually, communication is at the *center* of teaching. Teachers must be good communicators. This is so obvious that I hesitated even to write it down.

Yet, the meaning of this sentence is great. It is impossible to teach alone; we depend on the other person. If we want to be successful in our teaching, we must rely on the *other person's willingness and availability* to learn.

As teachers, we don't have to re-invent the wheel; there is a lot of good work on communication already at our disposal. I present to you mostly content I learned in therapy training, combined with core elements of pedagogy. Some ideas are from the non-violent communication framework. All this is pieced together using findings from cognitive science, especially the theory of joint cooperative action.

To teach well, we must properly "read" the other person. We must try to understand and be open. Our roles as teachers switch with dizzying speed. Within moments we must be able to change our attitude from instructor to counselor, from guide to psychologist.

This can be quite overwhelming.

I would like to offer some help in this regard. In the following part, you find explained the basic concepts of empathy, validation, and acceptance. You will also get sentences and questions at hand, ready for direct use in your teaching.

Chapter 15

"How Do I Reach Across?"
Interaction & Resources

Teaching is not an individual matter. Even if you record a YouTube-video, you are teaching something. You may be alone while doing that, but nonetheless, you imagine a potential viewer, a person watching it. You present your knowledge in a way that suits the needs and understanding of this (imagined) person.

So, teaching is *interaction*.

Interaction is fundamentally based on the idea of exchange. From an economic point of view, it's about exchanging *value*. You interact with someone because you want to receive something - it can be material or immaterial. If you go to a coffee shop, your goal is to get a coffee. You interact with the cashier there; you give money, you get coffee; it's simple.

Your coffee is a very hands-on type of value. Sometimes the values we get are more spiritual in nature. For example, you talk to an elderly lady on the street because she looks lonely. That's an act of kindness on your part. Nevertheless, you also get value out of it. You may feel good about yourself, or you do it because you remember your own grandma, or you want to fulfill your boy-scout vows.

The point is that interaction often involves an exchange of something of value. You may see that as a trade-off. In a best-case scenario, both sides come out on top - a *win-win-situation*. You give the cashier money and receive a coffee. (Hopefully, the coffee is of good quality and worth the money you spend.)

Teachers lead interactions; they are leaders in that sense. Even if seemingly passive, they lead through the network of formal and informal connections to their students. By leading, I do not mean leadership solely based on outward authority. Having been in the army, I can tell you that this is the least effective form of leadership. I mean a leader-follower-relationship by choice (in fancy terms, voluntary).

Voluntary leader-follower-relationships exist everywhere. They are most likely a product of social evolution. They involve an exchange (of information, coordination, services), which is good for both sides. Teachers (as leaders in this sense) can help students a lot, but it's not a one-way street. They also gain a lot, for example, personal reputation, influence, meaning, etc.[1]

People tend to avoid interactions that are not *beneficial* to them. I'm convinced that some kind of win-win-situation should be the norm, not the exception of human interactions. That's no dewy-eyed romanticism on my part. I believe that these situations are the most reliable basis for middle to long-term success together.

Sometimes, you stick it out, and you stay in a situation that is not good for you. Mostly that's a sign that there is a different ulterior motive involved. For example, you may be forced to tolerate the ravings of an abusive boss because you have financial responsibilities to your family. In this case, your ways of action are limited. But (if free to go) you would most probably leave.

In teaching, we should aim for win-win situations as often as possible. If people have a genuine benefit by interacting with you, they will be motivated to stay (more on this later). If we can truly understand what motivates the other person, then we have a chance to address these needs.

If the other's needs are met, they will be much more willing to listen to us and be open to what we try to convey. People seek relationships where they benefit, and if I benefit myself also, so much the better!

Teaching needs cooperation in order to be successful.

That's true for a lot of activities. Even in competitive sports, you need to cooperate. By working against each other, you essentially cooperate. Imagine a football game and one team declines to play ball. Of course, the other team wins, but it's no fun at all![2]

How is cooperation achieved? How do single actions intermesh? And how does interaction get a mutual goal? These questions are relatively new in science. Historically, scientists used to focus on the single brain. Roughly since the millennium, *collective activities* entered the focus of science. (In psychology, that was also the time when *mentalization* became a thing).

Interestingly, not all collective actions are on purpose. If you are stuck in a traffic jam, you most likely don't want to be there. Still, it's impossible to be in a traffic jam on your own - others have to be there. You get stuck by coincidence because too many people are on the street at the same time. Yet, you have no intention to do so.[3]

Many things people do purposefully can only be done as *joint activities* - team sports, ballroom dancing, chess, communication, the list is endless. Mutual support and cooperation are fundamental for all of them. Stanford scientist Bratman calls these types of activities "joint cooperative actions."

"Joint cooperative" means that the people involved are responsive to each other. They must be committed to the activity and to supporting each other. None of these three things (responsiveness, commitment, mutual support) is sufficient in and of itself. If we want to carry a couch together and I do not respond to you, we will fail. You may slightly shift your angle to adjust the weight, but If I drop the couch, then we will both have failed.[4]

Doing something together is (as scientists say) based on our individual mental and bodily faculties. If we carry a couch together, it's better if (1) I can see, (2) I'm strong, and (3) I can somehow talk with you and understand your directions. So, in order to better fit together, we use some sort of communication in most cases.

What's the difference between you and me taking a walk together and you and me walking side by side by chance? Obviously, walking together takes a lot more coordination; we must have the same pace, the same direction. And we must share the intention of going for a walk together. It has a *different quality* than passing each other on the street.

If we walk together, we decide to do so. There is an intention behind it; it's a joint cooperative action. The same applies to teaching. As teachers, we need a great deal of cooperation to reach our goals. I can try my best with state-of-the-art methods, but if students aren't willing and motivated to learn, there's hard to no progress.

For centuries, thinking about communication and language was focused only on the person speaking. Scientists looked at speech mainly as a means to say something - a tool to relate to the world. Not as a way of achieving something. Now we know (as Clark put it) that "language is used for doing things."[5] Language and any type of communication is *joint cooperative action.*

It's as impossible to communicate alone as executing a team maneuver in soccer or basketball. You need others to do so. While doing that, it's not a given that others understand your meaning immediately. We need to *work* to establish shared meanings.

Shared meanings are essential for understanding each other. Already Wittgenstein spoke about communication as a language game ("Sprachspiel"). It boils down to this - we have to find common ground. And common ground doesn't happen by accident; it must be established.[6]

If common ground is there, we share *meanings*. Our conversation has points of reference we both have. If we say a word, the other person has a reasonable assumption of what I might mean. This looks simple when applied to things like "table" or "spoon," but it's much harder with abstract terms as "liberty" or relative measures like "near," "close to," or "next to."

Successful communication is a joint cooperative action. If our goal is to reach some sort of understanding with the other person, then we can reach this goal only together. I'm convinced that inner strength is needed. We must be strong to be able to *really meet* the other person and, particularly, to be able to listen deeply, not superficially.

It's important to actively involve yourself with the other's inner world, especially at the beginning of working together. This is absolutely necessary to establish good contact and trust. *Contact* is the best basis to accompany and guide other people responsively and help them achieve their goals. Even when addressing a classroom full of students, you forge relationships with every single one of them.[7]

As teachers, we often make the fundamental mistake of assuming that other people are all *basically okay*. The opposite is true. It is important to remember that the other persons may have gone through challenging stages in their lives. Everyone suffers. They may have had negative experiences with attachment and relationships. It's possible that they are very sensitive and react strongly to any message or action, which can be understood or interpreted as *rejection* or *abandonment*.

Even when addressing a classroom full of students, you forge relationships with every single one of them.

In this regard, it's key to radiate warmth, competence, confidence, and the willingness to act. These traits help the other person to feel secure and safe. This may seem obvious, but please look critically at how you communicate, especially at your non-verbal communication.

As Watzlawick said, we are always communicating.[8] It's impossible not to communicate. Even if you are silent, your silence communicates something. (For example, the desire not to engage in conversation.) Often, we focus too much on what we say and too little on how we *behave.*

I firmly believe that the way we behave is a much stronger statement than anything we actually say. Students are very sensitive towards this - they analyze whether teachers are *consistent* and *authentic.* Both are tough standards to fulfill. If I preach understanding and responsivity but behave abusively towards my students, the message of my actions will be much stronger than my words.

I believe it was Viktor Frankl who remarked that values could not be taught - they can only be shown by example. How we are as teachers greatly influences how much we can achieve in class. This core belief of mine is also the reason why I so strongly suggest engaging in some sort of mental hygiene. The more stable you are inside, the more flexible you become in your responses in difficult situations.

To build trust and rapport, you can use some techniques. (I will sketch them in the following chapters.) But if they remain techniques, you are missing the point. I believe that many of these techniques only fulfill their full potential if used on the basis of genuine empathy and respect. You may discover during the process that the other person is actually very similar to yourself. And you may also find that you both need to work *together* to reach your *individual* goals; if you realize this, you've taken a very important step.

It's beneficial for building rapport to try to focus on the other person's gestures, poise, rhythm, cadence, and style of speaking first. We can learn a lot about the other person from these little hints already and sense the general state the other is in. We can sense a lot if we are curious! Let's engage with others with curiosity, which also means to refrain from *quick judgment.* That's unbelievably hard and a long process, and I'm always amazed at how quick I am to judge and to jump to conclusions.

There is a lot of talk about problem-orientation vs. solution-orientation. I think that's the wrong angle. We should aim for *resource-orientation.* Resources are where change comes from - only if we have enough inner resources can we effectively work for change.

We all have resources at our disposal, and they are our strengths, competencies, successes, and interests. It's imperative to activate these in teaching. Teachers often do this too little. If we focus too much on deficiencies, we fail to give the students hope for change. If we boost hope without a reality check, we raise unrealistic expectations. A well-balanced approach between focussing on problems and activating resources will yield the best results.[9]

Resources are the positive leverage we have to meet our basic needs. We have external resources (like advice by the teacher) and internal resources. Many students expect lessons to be mainly about correcting their mistakes, but that's wrong. As teachers, we need to work with the strengths a student has to offer. The student's qualities, skills, successes are the most important resource for change.

If I'm aware of my individual resources, I feel I can basically help myself. This activation of resources happens *within* the educational relationship. It also occurs through the academic relationship. The *quality* of the relationship is already a key resource. When communicating with students, we can build and rebuild resources. It is crucial to go *with* the feeling, not to talk too much *about* it.

That may sound too much like therapy to you.

You may be thinking, "Hey, I'm a teacher, not a psychotherapist! What's that to do with me?" That's certainly true - you are first and foremost a teacher. But the fact of the matter is, we always have different roles. In a single day, we go through a lot of roles. We are teachers, students, mothers, boyfriends, and professionals — why not add another function?

Why not learn from psychotherapy about how to help others to make meaningful changes in their lives? We have many different roles with very different sets of rules. Some of them are informal, some are professional. A professional role is different as there are formal rules to be obeyed. A professional relationship rests on a legal basis; if I violate this basis, I can be subjected to legal action.

The problem (and also the beauty) is that we are not machines. As teachers, we are in a *partly diffuse relationship* with our students.[10] They are diffuse, un-concrete because we are in it with our whole being. Our emotions, dreams, ambitions, anxieties influence how we behave.

Strictly speaking, these aspects do not belong in a professional relationship, but they tend to slag over into our professionalism. Formal interaction is intertwined with informal elements by its nature. It cannot be avoided.

This is the case because communication in class is never limited to technical exchange - there is always a relational component. As Watzlawick argues, the relational component is always *stronger* than the factual content.[11]

It's vital to be aware of the asymmetry of the situation. In teaching, there is a hierarchy. We have one side, which is (mostly) *older,* (hopefully) more *knowledgeable,* and (all being well) *interested* in helping the other side to excel. Teachers possess by definition an advantage over students. They are different in their levels of knowledge and power.

As a teacher, the question is, "How do you use this power?" Even if you intend to treat your students as equals, it's still *you* as a teacher who defines the exchange.[12] You can never entirely avoid the dilemma; a student's freedom is a concession by the system. That's the reason why we need formalized rules for conduct.

On top of these formal rules, we as teachers also need to be *scientifically informed*; our actions should be led by *established theory* and a *culture of skepticism.*[13] This may seem like an obvious requirement, but in reality, a lot of teaching is done on the basis of outmoded theories. I can understand that it's a great task to stay at the height of the professional discussion. It takes a lot of time, and it's tiring. But (on the upside) it offers us the chance to be up to date in our daily work.

Teachers and students are not friends; nor should they be. Their exchange can be *cordial*, but it's not a friendship. This relatively simple rule has far-reaching consequences. Many problems occur when the nature of a relationship is unclear. If I'm unclear about the relationship's inner nature, the danger is great to *project*. Projection comes easy if I (unconsciously) treat the other person as a friend, family member, or partner.

A good starting point is to define borders for the relationship. Educational relationships should be *goal-oriented* and *time-limited*. When I tell this to my students, the reactions vary. In some cases, I realize that saying so was the right thing to do.

We tend to avoid thinking about the ends of relationships, and it's not comfortable. The truth is that every relationship will end. When you offer a *secure attachment* to students, it's important to actively define the end of the relationship. The ending needs to be consciously managed. By doing so, you can give the student a last well-meaning impulse.

We often have problems with endings. The temptation is great to provoke a fight (usually regarding trivial matters) to make the pain of separation more bearable. Therefore, I recommend starting early to say that the educational relationship is limited in time - it will end sooner or later.

Since educational relationships are diffuse naturally, it's important to point out the differences between friendships and teacher-student-relationships. Friendships are open, not structurally time-limited, and symmetrical (at least in theory). In contrast, educational relationships are focused on *achieving something*. We want to reach a goal, and our topic is to reach this goal together.

For many students, this is a radical thought. We tend to interpret new relationships based on the ones we already know, especially the *mode* of relationship we already know. I often sense in the beginning that students don't exactly know how to assess their relationship with me. Am I a friend? A brother? A father? (These being the most common known modes of interaction.)[14]

The following chapter will dig deeper into the educational relationship and how it can be shaped.

Important points to remember

✓ Interaction often involves an exchange of something of value. In teaching, we should aim for win-win situations as often as possible. If people have a genuine benefit by interacting with us, they will be motivated to stay.

✓ Many things people do purposefully can only be done as joint activities. Language and any type of communication are collective, cooperative actions.

✓ As teachers, we are in a partly diffuse relationship with our students. We need to be scientifically informed and led by established theory.

✓ Teacher-student-relationships are not friendships. They are goal-oriented and time-limited.

Chapter references

1   For more information, see this article: Price, Michael E., VanVugt, Mark (2014): "The evolution of leader – follower reciprocity: the theory of service-for-prestige." Frontiers in Human Neuroscience, 8 363.

2   In fact, even examples of competitive or aggressive behavior (e.g., in sports) can be termed cooperative because there is a mutual result. As Searle remarks, a highly accomplished degree of cooperation is needed so one person can insult another at a cocktail party (see Searle 2009, 116).

3   Tuomela makes this case most convincingly in Tuomela, Raimo/ Miller, Kaarlo (2009): Wir-Absichten. Schmid, Hans Bernhard/ Schweikard, David P. (Hrsg.) (2009): *Kollektive Intentionalität. Eine Debatte über die Grundlage des Sozialen*. Frankfurt/ Main: Suhrkamp Verlag, 72-98.

4   For more information, see Bratman (2004, 95).

5   See Clark (2005, 3).

6   Clark stresses that "common ground isn't just there, ready to be exploited" (2005, 116).

7   More on this in my 2015 book Experts as *Effective Teachers*.

8   For more information, see Watzlawick, Paul, Beavin Bavelas, Janet, Jackson, Don D. (2011): *Pragmatics of Human Communication: A Study of Interactional Patterns, Pathologies and Paradoxes*. New York: W. W. Norton & Company.

9   See Gassmann & Grawe (2006).

10   See Oevermann (2009, 148).

11   This is one of Watzlawick's famous axioms: "Every communication has a content and relationship aspect such that the latter classifies the former." For more information, I would like to refer to:
Watzlawick, Paul, Beavin Bavelas, Janet, Jackson, Don D. (2011): Pragmatics of Human Communication: A Study of Interactional Patterns, Pathologies and Paradoxes. New York: W. W. Norton & Company.

12   See Dassler (1999, 96-97).

13   If you are interested in this, I would like to very strongly recommend reading David
Deutsch (2011): *The Beginning of Infinity: Explanations That Transform the World.* London: Penguin.

14   Noticeably, teachers are often likened to parents, especially male teachers to fathers. As
one example among many, Kloss writes in her book, "Jascha Heifetz Through My Eyes" about
her studies, recalling that her teacher had a striking resemblance to her father, both outwardly
and by his inner nature. She describes the violinist as acting as an "intuitive parent." (2000, 71)

Chapter 16

"Close encounters"
Shaping the Educational Relationship

As a teacher, I have to lead the educational relationship; I must shape it. It's clear that the asymmetry and hierarchy involved obliges me to take a leading role. The interaction modes we already know (sibling, parent, friend, etc.) tempt us to get back to them. I (as a teacher) must help the student to develop a new model of interaction. This mode can be something entirely new: "Teacher offering secure attachment."

From a professional point of view, it's good to have a two-tier approach. On the one hand, I'm an *expert* in my field, and on the other hand, I act as a significant other, a *trusted partner*. I form the relationship with the student to allows us to collaborate in the best way possible, openly and actively. Teacher and student are in an *alliance*.

As a teacher, I must motivate, support, activate, and inform. It's important to discuss in the beginning what expectations exist. If the student expects me to solve his or her problems *on my own*, we will not succeed as a *team*. We need to *collaborate* with input from both sides. I'm convinced that self-efficacy and self-esteem are built best through positive experiences. If I attribute my success to something I did myself, my self-esteem will rise. If I attribute my success to my teacher or coach, I will become dependent.

In psychotherapy, there are studies about personalities that show the client's personality forecasts success in roughly 30 percent of the cases.[1] The way we are influences whether a technique, an intervention, or a strategy will succeed. We all have attachment styles typical to us. Students with secure attachment tend to have positive relationships with their teachers. And positive relationships translate into educational success (as a general rule).

Likewise, teachers have an attachment style. It can be the case that the student is securely attached, but the teacher isn't! There is the danger that the teacher will try (subconsciously) to heal his or her attachment deficits with the student. In my biography, I met teachers who saw themselves as some kind of gurus. They groomed a certain reverence in their students. Today I think that's already over the line!

That's another reason why I recommend (at least) short-term psychotherapy for every teacher. The better you know yourself, the better you can help others. If you know your psyche well, you can be more professional. As part of our professionalism, we should try to embody the following traits in our practice:

- Positivity
- Goal-oriented
- Flexibility

Of course, we should be experts in our fields. Our behavior should be carried by sympathy, empathy, and pushing for *autonomy* on an emotional level. As a technique, autonomy can be fostered by offering small, manageable steps; this is called *shaping* in psychology.

Shaping is the *reinforcement* of behaviors, which leads to reaching a goal step-by-step. If a student is reluctant to start working on a paper, it can be useful to divide the task into little steps. Every small step offers the opportunity for a reward. We must know our students well to be able to do that competently. We must know where their limits are, which task poses a manageable barrier, and which task needs to be broken down into smaller bits. We must accept our students, know them, and also have a certain professional distance. It's delicate!

More generally, the question is, "How do we see students?" Do we see them as *lacking*? Do they need us to give them something? I don't think so. I'm convinced that (typically) human beings carry the tools they need within themselves. As a teacher, I try to help students discover a wealth of possible solutions. If I don't do that, there is the danger that students will become dependent on me.

Autonomy and independence are my goals; I must help the students to embrace a basic attitude of *experiment and research*. I strongly believe that the greatest achievement, the achievement with the most significant long-term yield, is to motivate students to look at problems from the viewpoint of scientific explanation. We try out explanations. We test them. And if they hold the test, great! If they don't, we go on searching.

The most effective help is always enabling people to help themselves; it's the old *self-help approach*. As teachers, we are no longer telling others what, when, and how to do things. Rather, we are guides, offering support and attendance. We provide a safety net, confidence, and help for the students on their journey. Ultimately, learning is a *self-discovery* and a process of development.

Think about physiotherapy - physiotherapy aims not to treat the patient for years, but rather, physiotherapy tries to analyze the pain and its causes. Then physiotherapists work with the patient to better cope with pain, find better solutions, avoid strain, etc. It's goal-oriented and time-limited.

As I said, the teacher-student-relationship is asymmetrical. But this asymmetry does not mean that the teacher is never allowed to share personal information. For example, a student is entitled to know how and where the teacher gained their expertise. That's professional information, not personal information in and of itself.

Other than that, it can help the student to learn some degree of personal information about the teacher. Professionally, this is called *self-revelation*. Self-revelation is offering a carefully managed degree of personal information. Sharing personal information makes me *vulnerable,* and a consciously offered vulnerability can be a powerful tool to shift the balance within the relationship.

By carefully revealing some personal information, I can try to boost the students' trust in me. I can also try to lessen the power imbalance. If I open up a little bit, students feel that they know me better; I'm easier to trust. In my case, when students know that I have a three-year-old daughter, they tend to look at me differently. In psychology, this technique is called *controlled self-disclosure.*

Controlled self-disclosure can be about something in my private life. It can also be something as simple as my personal reactions. Reactions are a very important feedback mode in interactions - my responses are the *first form* of feedback. Before I even voice something (praise, criticism), my face and my body language already hint at the mood I'm in. My reactions offer insight into my inner self.

Offering this insight into myself makes me vulnerable, and people could use this knowledge against me. For example, if my face shows "anger" in a given situation, people could use this knowledge to set me off with intention.

On the other hand, vulnerability is a great tool to boost empathy within the other person. If we show vulnerability (in a strategic and organized manner), we can change the other person's perception of us. In turn, this tends to influence the other's perception of him or herself. They may experience themselves as people worthy of trust or understand that other people have a private life too.

Sometimes, it can even be helpful to admit mistakes or to not knowing something. If the relationship is good and strong, admitting something like that can make it even stronger. In the end, all of this comes down to communication and feeling our way around the other person when we talk.

There is no perfect communication. If we are afraid of making mistakes, we will fail. We must face our own mistakes with courage. There is also no perfect teaching.

For students, perfectionist ideals quite often lie at the core of their psychological suffering. A seemingly perfect teacher would strengthen the belief that perfection is possible. (In psychology, this is called "mastery-model.") Instead, a teacher should embody a "coping-model," getting along with your deficits, problems, and mistakes. To see the teacher coping with difficulties teaches the students that coping is *possible* and a *necessary* fact of life - because perfectionism is unattainable.

Teachers help students to reach their goals by offering paths to rid obstacles on the way to achievement. Of course, the teachers' own personality influences how they communicate. We always make choices when speaking and listening. What do I say? How do I act? Am I listening closely? Or rather superficially?

As teachers, our actions should always be aimed at helping the other. One technique I already talked about is controlled self-disclosure. Self-disclosure is designed to help the other, not to unburden me. It's a *technique* to help the student. If I use this technique, I do so *without giving up control*. Don't confuse it with telling the student your problems or the story of your life. If I need help, I must seek it at the appropriate places.

It is crucial that teachers know profoundly what their own needs are. I need to know my own personal situation and *behavior patterns*; only when I know them can I judge correctly how I feel towards a student - and why and what I feel. Actually, it happens frequently to me that I see myself in a student. Many students experience situations in their lives similar to what I've gone through.

It's dangerous to identify with students and their problems too much. If you do so, there is a lack of boundaries. This doesn't sound too bad, but you see that this can lead to *asking too much* of yourself when you analyze it deeper. I often wonder if there is a need within me to be seen by others as a special person. If you want to be seen as special and superhuman in your strengths, this can lead to burn-out and self-sacrifice.[2]

Self-sacrifice is a difficult matter. Teaching is a job, which never ends,[3] and we need to address our own perfectionism. That's the reason why I strongly suggest supervision and psychotherapy for teachers. Supervision can help better understand your inner motivations and patterns. It can prevent projections. As teachers, we need productive psychological self-care.[4]

As pointed out in the last chapter, teachers and students form an *alliance*. It's an alliance because neither can fulfill their goals without the other. More often than not, teachers fail to talk about goals with their students, but discussing them is necessary. Otherwise, success can not be measured from either side! Only if a clear goal structure is established can progress be assessed.

Another thing most teachers don't talk about is *mutual expectations*. What do I expect from the student? What may the student expect from me? Goals, expectations, and the relationship's affective side form a triangle, and these three parameters influence each other. A good relationship (with secure attachment) can strengthen the students' motivation; it helps make them open for technical input. In a securely attached relationship, the students' resources and needs are an important tool for progress.[5] "Lift up, don't put down." That would be a great guiding principle. In my opinion, teachers can learn a lot from psychotherapy. The main difference I see is that therapy is intended to *heal*. In therapy, there is a pathology, a disease.

In a securely attached relationship, the students' resources and needs are an important tool for progress. "Lift up, don't put down". That would be a great guiding principle.

Diseases need to be healed. But what counts as a disease? The definition is quite loose, and roughly speaking, it's a disease if a patient is *suffering*. For me, this was a revelation. Many students I encounter suffer a lot.

Some of them can't sleep, some have problems with eating, and some have intense anxiety and stress. When they see me for counseling, we talk about their problems. We try to find the right strategies, and often, the border to therapy is hard to see. Nevertheless, teachers can learn from therapy settings — but they aren't therapists. Nor should they be.

Pedagogy is not therapy; teachers aren't therapists. They shouldn't have to *heal* their students. Preferably, pedagogy (at its best) has the ability to work towards *prevention*. Pedagogy is aimed at learning new skills, new behaviors, new perspectives. While doing that, I can try to help the student gain new perspectives on their identity. That's a byproduct of the primary learning process.

Our identity is in constant construction. We build it based on the experiences we made, the skills we have, and the emotions we live through. At the core, all of this is somehow accomplished on a neural level because of the brain's ability to reorganize itself (*synaptic plasticity*) while aspects of our identity change.

We can change aspects of how we see ourselves. We can alter how we feel about ourselves. When I learn a new skill, the way I see myself changes on a very subtle level: Before I couldn't do something, now I can. That's a big change - I experience myself as being able to do something. When I learn a new skill, my feeling of self-efficacy is enhanced.[6]

We can learn from therapy — while not forgetting that we are first and foremost teachers. A good example is *goal-orientation*. Therapy, especially cognitive behavioral therapy, is always goal-oriented. Therapy is designed to help the client to reach his or her goals.[7] That's also a very good approach for pedagogy. In the beginning, goals should be formulated and measurable in a specific way: attractive (to boost motivation), realistic, and within a specific time frame.

I recommend discussing goals in class - many teachers fail to do so. Goal-orientation (as opposed to competitiveness) is a significant key to motivation.[8] To establish goals is an excellent opportunity to focus on goal-oriented teaching versus competitiveness. We know that competition as a motivational driver is very powerful. Still, it has many adverse effects - competitiveness tends to bind a lot of energy.

To speak about goals is important, but goals are not set in stone - it is crucial to stay flexible. There should be enough freedom to change them when necessary. Along the process, it might become apparent that other goals are more important than the ones chosen in the beginning.

One method is to use a "technique of a million steps" (shaping). Even the most complex changes must be broken down into chewable bits. As the old Chinese saying goes, "Even a walk of a thousand miles starts with the first step." Every step on the way is a success; better is good.[9] There is nothing more successful than success itself. Every step taken is a success, and every success is a chance to boost self-esteem and self-efficacy.

Teachers help students to feel the ropes - they offer encouragement and criticism. Students need to feel that they are on the right track. To accomplish this, clear tasks must be formulated for both sides. I have good experiences with asking students to develop the job they would like me to do. When students tell me what they expect me to do, they "hire" me, so to speak. Psychologically, this does two things: first, they feel in *charge*, and second, they understand on a profound level that I'm only a *helper* in this process. *They* must put in the work to reach the goal.

Many teachers don't do that. Initially, that's not a problem, but later, problems tend to occur. If we don't discuss goals and strategies, there is a paternalistic undercurrent to the ensuing teaching. It's like the teacher saying, "I know what's good for you, and you don't." Discussing goals establishes a sense of cooperation. I'm astonished time and time again when I start talking about goals with students. More often than not, I learn that I had a completely wrong idea of what the student wanted or needed. The student's goal can be quite different from what I think it is.

A paternalistic attitude can be comfortable for the student initially - it's nice to feel being taken care of. Nevertheless, later in the process, problems often surface. The student may feel misunderstood, disrespected, or manipulated, which can lead to a lot of resistance and passivity.

Discussing goals shows the student that he or she has to be active. Goals also show that *change is possible*. At the beginning of this book, I quoted David Deutsch. For me, it was a big revelation to understand that everything is possible (physics permitting) if the right *knowledge* is there. If we know, we can change. If we can change, it's our responsibility to do so; or take on the responsibility if we don't.

It's easy to blame something on the outside world. It's much harder to admit that I lack the knowledge to solve a problem - that the problem, therefore, rests within *me*.

You already know I'm a musician. Here's an example from violin playing - I have long fingers. If I do vibrato on the violin, as described in the books, the result is an unpleasant sound. I always had the goal of having a better-sounding, nicer vibrato. Goals such as this forced me to formulate *specifically* and *realistically*. It took me a long time to understand that I cannot change the length of my fingers — but I can actively search for better technical solutions. Better solutions then allow me to bring my internal idea of sound into outside reality.

How can this be accomplished in the classroom? A good affective relationship makes it easier for the student to change. I've already stated that change is hard. Change is a risk. Therefore, the *quality* of relationships is of the greatest importance.[10] If I feel I can trust my teacher, if I hope for things to get better and feel positive and competent with him or her, then change comes *easier*.

Important points to remember

✓   As teachers, we are in a partly diffuse relationship with our students. Teacher and student are in an alliance. As a teacher, I must motivate, support, activate, and inform, so students gain autonomy and independence.

✓   Learning is a self-discovery and a process of development.

✓   Self-revelation means offering a carefully managed degree of personal information.

✓   Pedagogy is aimed at learning new skills, new behaviors, and new perspectives.

✓   Discussing goals establishes a sense of cooperation. Goals should be measurable in a specific way: attractive (to boost motivation), realistic, and within a specific time frame.

Chapter references

1   See Norcross & Lambert, 2011.

2   In psychotherapy, it's been clear for quite some time how important it is to know your own styles, patterns, and vulnerabilities. See for reference: Haarhoff B. (2006): "The importance of identifying and understanding therapist schema in cognitive therapy training and supervision." *New Zealand Journal of Psychology*, 35,126–131.

3   Sue Cowley points this out in great clarity in Cowley, Sue (2009): *Teaching Skills for Dummies*. Chichester: John Wiley & Sons, Ltd.

4   From a psychotherapy perspective, you can find suitable srategies here: Lohmann B. (2017): *Selbstunterstützung für Psychotherapeuten*. Göttingen: Hogrefe.

5   This framework is used in therapy for decades. For reference: Bordin E. S. (1979): "The generalizability of the psychoanalytic concept of the working alliance." *Psychotherapy: Theory, Research & Practice*, 16, 252–260.

6   The seminal text in this regard is Bandura's: *Principles of behavior modification*. New York: Holt, Rinehart and Winston, from 1969.

7   This is a basic concept. It can be found e.g. here: Schulte D. (1996): *Therapieplanung*. Göttingen: Hogrefe.

8   See Schunk, Dave H., Pintrich, Paul R., Meece, Judith L. (2013): *Motivation in education: Theory, research and applications*. Upper Saddle River, N.J.: Pearson Education International.

9   I first heard this from Pres. Obama – but I don't know if he invented this saying or not.

10   This is also a concept often formulated in psychotherapy guidelines; see, for example, Schulte (1996).

Chapter 17

Entering the Digital Age: What Does It Mean for Teaching?

In a nutshell, the core argument of this book thus far is:

> Learning is autopoiesis: It needs motivation. As teachers, we can try to
> guide students through the process. We can help to navigate obstacles,
> show possible shortcuts, and offer advice. All this has to be done in a
> positive affective relationship because a positive learning climate greatly
> facilitates learning. A positive affective relationship can be built through
> communication.

As I said in the previous chapter, the quality of relationships is of the greatest
importance for success in teaching. Risking to be soon outdated, I think it's safe
to say that we are on the brink of a new age. Digital media change communication
patterns rapidly.

Never in the history of humanity has change been as rapid. As with many new
technologies, it takes time to really understand the effect they have on society.
When steam engines were invented, no one knew how they would change the face
of the world.

The same is true with the digital age. I still remember the beginnings of the
internet; I remember when the first webcam was used to monitor a coffee machine.
Never in my wildest dreams did I imagine the impact all this would have on all of
us. We live in the digital age, but we still can't really see the extent to which change

will happen in the near future.

The Corona pandemic of 2020 (Covid-19) has shown the direction these processes will most likely take. Due to necessary lockdowns, millions of working people worked from home. They used many different platforms on the internet to conduct online meetings and conferences - the home office became normal in a very short period of time.

As far as education is concerned, this accelerated many developments, which were already taking place before. Now, they took on lightning speed. Within weeks, online teaching became the norm. Even if we could go back to some normality (before Covid-19), it is more likely that these developments will stay. New contracts are already drawn up by schools and universities, allowing for online teaching in a "normal" time without legal problems.

It is safe to say that teaching digitally will be part of our educational system more and more in the future.[1]

How will this affect teaching? The way we teach? How can we use existing best practices (like investing in reliable educational relationships) and transfer them to the digital age? Is it possible? Which changes are necessary?

I will admit that I was always reluctant about digital teaching. I tended to see online teaching as a less desirable option. It seemed to me that it can be done, but I thought it *should* only be done if outside factors make face-to-face teaching impossible (because of long distances, for example).

As with many discussions, which start as purely academic discourse and are then overtaken by events, Covid-19 made this train of thought obsolete. The question is not whether we like online teaching; it simply *is* part of our profession's future. I'm immensely grateful that the internet exists - imagine this pandemic *without* the digital means at our disposal nowadays.

In this book, I lay out what I understand to be necessary to build positive, productive educational relationships through communication. Now, we must look at the options the internet gives us in order to transport this into the digital age.

The good news is that it can be done. We can build reliable relationships also via the internet. To do so, we need some fundamental requirements to be met. These requirements may be basic, but they are by no means simple. You need sufficient bandwidth, for example. You need some sort of quiet room on both ends of the interaction. And you need adequate technology (internet access, computers, microphones, lights, and a good webcam) in place to work effectively. It may sound basic, but in poorer communities, it's not a given.

If these basic requirements are established, you can start to look at the interaction itself. In psychotherapy, there is already a body of scientific research on the topic. It's clear - Internet-based therapy is effective.[2]

Studies show that the media you use is not crucial to success - it matters surprisingly little. It is the quality of the therapeutic relationship that determines the outcome.[3] It is possible to build a stable relationship via the internet. When you compare face-to-face interactions with digital formats, the digital relationship is assessed positively *to a similar degree*. So, the difference isn't so significant after all.

I'm convinced that all the tools and techniques discussed in this book can also be used online. You can very well focus on basic psychological needs. You can try to understand motivations. And you can try to boost self-efficacy. All this is possible.

The challenge I see is that attention and focus are harder to maintain. As a teacher, you have less control. Students can easily do something else while you try to explain something without you having a clue.

I find that the amount of energy I have to use to keep lessons on track is markedly higher than in face-to-face teaching. It seems to me that the overall academic outcome is less - in a rough ballpark number, I would say that about 70-80% of what you can achieve face-to-face with the same amount of time.

The main problem for building a stable, effective working relationship is that online teaching reduces emotionality[4] because you interact with a camera, and non-verbal and behavioral signals are less. Sprick (rather off-handedly) states that there are no non-verbal and behavioral signals. I disagree; I think they are simply *reduced in volume.*

If you teach through digital media, you have to learn to treat the camera like an audience - actors and actresses have been doing that for a long time. I recommend reading Chubbuck's excellent "The Power of the Actor."[5] This will give insight into how acting professionals prepare for performing on camera. It's good to do some trial runs - record yourself and analyze. You will see very quickly what works well and what doesn't. (There is a lot of advice on these matters available online.)

If you develop your on-screen persona, you can very effectively build stable educational relationships also online. It's good to work on these qualities. In the future, it will be more and more of a requirement (in my opinion). On-screen or off-screen, learning to communicate effectively and circumspectly is very important. The next chapters will focus on how to achieve this.

Important points to remember

✓   Teaching digitally will be part of our educational system more and more in the future.

✓   Studies show that the media you use is not crucial to success - they matter surprisingly little.

✓   The main problem for building a stable, effective working relationship is that online teaching reduces emotionality - learn from acting professionals in this regard.

Chapter references

1   See A. W. (Tony) Bates (2019): *Teaching in a Digital Age. Guidelines for designing teaching and learning*. Vancouver: BCcampus.

2   See Andersson (2009).

3   See Sucala M., Schnur J.B., Constantino M.J., Miller S.J., Brackman E.H. & Montgomery G.H. (2012): "The therapeutic relationship in e-therapy for mental health: A systematic review." Journal of Medical Internet Research, 14, e110.

4   see Sprick (2017).

5   See Chubbuck, Ivana (2004): *The Power of the Actor*. New York: Gotham Books.

Chapter 18

Communication Techniques and Respect

Learning means embracing change - entering the digital age shows us that. If I learn a new skill (a new dance step), I learn a new motion. To use this motion properly is *behavior*. To put new behavior into effect is behavioral change. I do something that I couldn't do before. I act in a way I wasn't able to earlier.

To embrace change, I need to trust the people who help me, but personal trust is not the same as trusting someone's competence.[1] Personal trust is an important resource to *reduce anxiety*. If I feel safe, secure, accepted, valued, and understood, I have less fear. To trust in the competence of my teacher means to believe that he or she will be able to help me effectively. (I can trust someone's competence and absolutely distrust them personally.)

But effective help is not a matter of technical expertise; it involves other traits like personality and resource-orientation. Teachers should look for the resources in their students. If they feel seen with their strengths and successes, they are more optimistic about their prospects. They need *emotional validation and acceptance*. As a student, it's important to experience understanding and sympathy from my teacher.

Sympathy is good. Without *transparency and cooperation*, it will be useless. There must be a clear agenda, and it must be apparent where the journey goes and how goals will be reached. Competence is to know about possible avenues of approach. It also means to be *willing* and *able* to modulate the process individually for the student. Sympathy and cooperation need reliability for success, and without reliability and consistency, hard-earned trust can be lost easily.

Learners have a strong sense of consistency and authenticity; they feel if I'm true or not. It's a good investment to build a reliable basis here. Investing in the teacher-student-relationship is like investing in a portfolio - the more you invest, the more you can withdraw when needed.

The more I invest in the relationship, the more I can expect from students when they face difficult situations (like exams, competitions). Many problems occur when there is no balance between hardship and relationships. On the other hand, we can bear a lot of difficulties when carried by a good relationship (to our teachers). I've seen it again and again - students can reach far beyond what they thought achievable when supported by a rock-like trust from their teacher.

Some behaviors are good for the investment: Others aren't.

For example, it's not helpful if I:

- Ask too many critical questions
- Confront students too often
- Show impatience

If I:

- Have no respect
- Don't care enough
- Use accusations

Or if I'm:

- Not flexible
- Controlling
- Not very interested

There is a funny study with psychotherapists. When you become a therapist, you must take therapy yourself. In this study, therapists (while in therapy themselves) felt that their therapists were indifferent and not empathetic in 30 percent of the cases![2]

A good relationship is key.

It's also hard to fake. That's why I recommend trying to *genuinely feel sympathy* for your students - they will know the difference. If you feel that they like you, you are on the right track. If you feel their respect and you respect them, it's great. If they show that they trust you with (little) stories from their lives, it's a good sign.

These stories are actually not just stories - they are the offer of a relationship. By opening up to you, your students implicitly say, "I accept you, and I reveal something about myself. Please value this gift." The best way to reciprocate is to show that you are true to the student.

Being true is easy when everything is smooth sailing. When things get rougher, it's a different matter. Your students need you, especially in failure. They need to know that you also hold true to them when it's not easy. In my own history, I still remember the feeling of abandonment when my teachers left me in the lurch immediately when things got tough. Please don't make this mistake - It's excruciating to feel abandoned in times of need.

What does all of this mean in every-day life?

Perhaps you're asking yourself, "It sounds good, but how do I actually do that?"

Let me show you the path I've taken. In my opinion, the most important point to understand is *cooperation* - teachers and students working together. Teaching is a joint-cooperative action (Bratman 2004). If you accept this argument, all adversarial thinking goes out of the window. You serve your best interest when you do whatever you can to help the other person.

Teachers serve their students. (I have a very positive definition of service.) As a teacher, I accept a task; I have a job. My job is to help the student to reach his or her goals. This implies that the student has to show responsibility also.

It's a very delicate balance. On the one hand, it has to be clear that meaningful change can only come through commitment; nothing worth-while in life comes easy. On the other hand, the student must reliably feel that the teacher is supportive and helpful — the teacher and student are equal partners in this process. The teacher, as an expert, offers guidance and support. Part of this support is reinforcing the student's self-efficacy and autonomy.

Practically speaking, it's helpful to suggest this in the language you choose. It's a big difference between saying, "Why didn't you do the assignment?" (accusatory), "What kept you from doing the assignment?" (more supportively), or "How could we have prepared better for the assignment?"

The teacher-student-relationship is cooperative and asymmetrical. The student offers his or her commitment, willingness to work, and talent. The teacher provides expertise, perspective, and structure. In this understanding, the teacher aims not to correct deficits (an often-encountered misconception); instead, it's about working out problems together.

Cooperation also means that I (as a teacher) admit that I *could* be wrong. We try out different strategies together based on the expertise and knowledge I have. By no means is it clear that my interventions will be successful - there is no guarantee.

Non-verbal communication is a crucial part of interpersonal contact. There is a lot of literature about building rapport - most of it I see rather critically. Mirroring the other person too much or parroting what he or she said will get you nowhere. From my point of view, it's much more valuable to focus on more general things:

- What's the mood like?
- How does the other person talk?
- Are there mannerisms? Favorite words? Keywords?

Quite often, people use keywords when describing an experience. Imagine a student talking to you about an exam, saying, "I was so nervous before, and then I walked into the room. I felt so unprepared; my whole brain went blank; I was devastated…"

The student actually offers you not only information here but many possible avenues of further inquiry. I would suggest listening for intonation and inflictions. Which words get special emphasis? Try to use words that the student stresses and repeat them in a similar manner (as a question). Most likely, the student will then elaborate, starting with the word you repeated.

In the above example, the student says, "I felt so unprepared." As a teacher, you can answer, "You felt unprepared?" The student might continue, "Yes, unprepared, and I don't know why! I learned a lot, but somehow there is no end to studying. It's never enough. I'm always anxious." Which you could reply, "There is no end to it?" and so on.

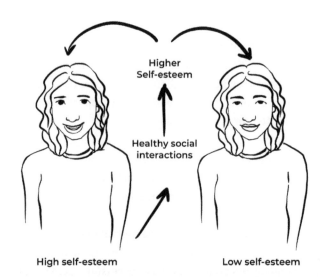

Empowerment grows from a feeling of autonomy. Empowerment boosts self-esteem:
Self-esteem in turn is boosted by healthy social interactions.

This technique, mirroring, actually has many layers; the main idea is *not to disturb* the psychological act in progress. You lead the interaction, but you do so by following the other. By asking questions, the resource (the topic at hand) is named again. We all have resources at our disposal; resources are the pulse of our life. Using them (and by not using them) shapes the trajectory of the experiences we have.

I firmly believe that the core of change is *empowerment,* meaning that I can actively work for observable change. Empowerment grows from a feeling of autonomy, and autonomy is closely linked to self-efficacy (the trust I have in my own abilities).

Self-efficacy has to be supported by teachers.

To do so, language use is crucial. Many students believe that they are their problems - that's not true. They have them. Therefore it's not good to say, "You are wrong in this." It's better to speak (for example) about "correcting false beliefs." If you ask me, "Why are you anxious?" the message I receive is, "I'm anxious, and that's the problem.: If you ask me, "How can you better manage your anxiety?" it's clear that I have a problem and (by implication) that it can be managed (externalizing the problem). It's always helpful to externalize problems.

Classically, teacher, student, and subject matter find themselves in a triangle. In this triangle, the teacher has the *process responsibility* - he or she manages and modulates the process and has oversight. The teacher offers structure, the "ropes" and is responsible for correctly managing the process. In my own experience, a surprising number of students crave *directiveness;* they like being told what to do. (Maybe because this reduces their responsibility?) In the Short-term, that may seem like an excellent strategy, but the long-term can lead to students depending on teachers too much.

Changing *yourself* is ultimately better than *being changed* by someone else - we call that *non-directiveness.* Part of this attitude of non-directiveness is transparency. Transparency means that I do not have a secret agenda. I'm open about what my stakes in the teaching process are.

Teachers and students should speak about it from time to time. In a transparent process, the student should know where he or she stands. The student should be able to explain to others (family, friends) what's going on. I strongly suggest that students "read around" (books, internet) to further a feeling of expertise. It can be uncomfortable for teachers to be confronted with a critical student, but a student on the path to expertise is already empowered!

Transparency is also a sign of respect. Respect is the fundamental belief that the other person is worthy as an individual. I respect his or her decisions. Not only should the student be respected for skills, performance, or problem-solving strategies, but it's vital that the student feels taken seriously, not taken advantage of, or patronized.

Respect is difficult when the decisions taken by the student go against my proposals as an expert. Autonomy means accepting the student's decisions even if they do not align with what I believe. It may sound counter-intuitive at first, but it's a good strategy; trust me, don't try to *push through* your points.

Instead:

- Retreat (step back from the conflict)
- Regroup (assess the resources at your disposal)
- Reduce resistance (more on this later)

Ask yourself, "What did the student just gain from going against my proposal?" (That opens up the motivational question.)

From the viewpoint of respect, it's necessary to offer a culture of benevolent critique in teaching - this cuts both ways. The student can professionally criticize the teacher. Being criticized is uncomfortable, but a good thing! It helps the teacher to get better at teaching. We are all part of a big system. We are not adversaries; we must work together to achieve what we aspire to.

Often, problems arise when criticism is worded in a manner that looks like a personal attack. Keeping Watzlawick in mind, it's clear that the emotional content is always dominant when we speak; therefore, the danger is great to misunderstand. We can easily affect others or be affected in turn. Never underestimate the power of "preservation of self-worth" — even well-meant criticism can be devastating.

Out of a need to protect self-worth, a lot of resistance can come. When we are criticized (by students), it's vital to react to this criticism *constructively*. This reaction in and of itself is already powerful teaching. The way we handle a situation of criticism is model-learning (Bandura's social-cognitive theory of learning). If we cope with criticism positively and productively, we embody the change we want to further. As Gandhi is alleged to have said, "Be the change you want to see in the world."

Practitioner's tip:
But what to say precisely? (I'm often tongue-tied under challenging situations; therefore, I find it handy to have a few sentences ready to go if needed.) In my opinion, here's a good response to use, "I have the feeling something is wrong. Please tell me what you just found disturbing."

When I feel attacked, I tend to entrench myself behind my professional expertise. I say then things like, "I have studied this thoroughly and thus..." (Not only does this sound awfully pompous, it's also a bad strategy.) It's a big difference whether you react to criticism by saying, "It seems you don't like this teaching" (counter-attack). Or whether you say, "It seems like the way I offer this teaching is not suitable for you" (defusing the situation).

Respect has to be given proactively. As experts in the field (and older partners in the process), we need to do it first. We cannot wait for students (who are in a weaker position in the hierarchy) to do so. I've encountered this many times - when bad behavior is a problem, there is mostly a lack of mutual respect at the core.

Disrespect has many faces. We always communicate, and it might not be overt disrespect or a general attitude of disdain, which translates into non-verbal communication. That's the reason why I believe it's so important to develop genuine sympathy for your students and their needs.

As I just stated, please don't underestimate the power of self-worth preservation. Strong resistance can result from the need to protect self-esteem; therefore, it's most important to offer criticism that leaves the self-worth of the student intact. Enhancing self-worth is a basic psychological need. To stress the point further, teachers *need* the students' willingness to accept change because it's always the student who changes. Understanding is autopoiesis by nature. Change will only come if the student understands the necessity to do so and is willing to go down that road.

If you want to challenge passivity, there are different suitable paths. You can choose to ask for more activity by appealing to the student's responsibility, or you can point out the resources at the student's disposal. You could say something like, "Someone with your level of skills/expertise/background has the chance to do something about this problem."

You can also try to reinforce every small instance of self-responsibility and initiative. You could say, "I find it remarkable how strongly you've shown that you don't want to do this. This shows that, in the end, you decide in which direction this is going." (This is a sneaky way of enhancing the other's feeling of responsibility.)

In my experience, passivity is often mixed with a negative self-view and a feeling of hopelessness - it has to be addressed slowly and in little steps. The problem is that sometimes students demonstrate strong confidence on the outside while being very unsure in reality. As a teacher, this demands intense mentalization. Often we need to work hard to see behind the superficial screen of demonstratively "strong" behavior.

Responsibility is not strengthened through pressure, threats, or accusations. Sentences like, "It's your life, and you must see for yourself how much you want to solve your problems" are not helpful. More often than not, sentences like these will make the student feel *ashamed*, under pressure, and anxious. This can lead to retreating from the educational relationship. Responsibility has to be taken on *willingly*. Confrontation will most likely not lead to the desired effect; a feeling of trust and positive cooperation will.

Trust and positive cooperation don't come overnight — they require a feedback culture. Feedback needs to be actively shaped and trained. As you already know, the teacher-student-relationship is partly diffuse and hierarchical. Therefore, feedback has to be initialized by the teacher. A framework has to be established, which gives the student license for benevolent criticism.

Feedback should be asked for regularly. Suitable questions include, "Are you content with how this is going? Are we getting closer to our goals? Are you happy with the results so far?" Another line of inquiry could be, "What would you like to do more (or less)? Would you like to take different steps/techniques?" Or, on a more relational basis, "Do you feel understood and accepted by me? Do you trust me?"

Feedback in and of itself is a relationship intervention. Studies have shown that in therapy settings, merely asking for feedback already has a positive effect. Feedback is essential because our assessment of a relationship is notoriously unreliable. If you fail to establish a relationship allowing feedback, you are in danger of missing important cues about potential disagreements - you risk a worsening emotional climate. The result may very well be lacking cooperation, resistance, and (in the end) a break-up of the educational relationship.

You already sense that these questions will only be effective if a proper working relationship with mutual trust and benevolence was previously established. I can't stress this often enough - investment into the relationship is key. Asking for feedback without a good relationship will not work. Most likely, you will only get what the other person *thinks* you *want* to hear.

Teachers should see themselves as change agents; we modulate a process, setting interventions, giving structure, and offering expertise. The educational system has demands towards us, and we are obliged to bring students to a certain level of expertise. Putting pressure on students feels like a good strategy, especially when we feel stressed, but in reality, there is a limit to coercion. If we push students against their will, we will not succeed long-term.

Important points to remember

✓   A good affective relationship makes it easier for the student to change. The core of change is empowerment.

✓   Investing in the teacher-student-relationship is like investing in a portfolio. The more you invest, the more you can withdraw when needed.

✓   Teaching is joint cooperative action. Teachers serve their students. The teacher-student-relationship is cooperative and asymmetrical.

✓   Respect is the fundamental belief that the other person is worthy as an individual.

✓   As teachers, we are change agents. We modulate a process, set interventions, give structure, and offer expertise.

Chapter references

1   As pointed out by Sachse R. (2015). *Therapeutische Beziehungsgestaltung*. Göttingen: Hogrefe.

2   This is the study: Curtis R., Field C., Knaan-Kostmann L., Mannis K. (2014): "What 75 psychoanalysts found helpful and hurtful in their own analysis." *Psychoanalytic Psychology*, 21, 183–202.

Chapter 19

To See through the Other's Eyes: Empathy and Change Orientation

Putting others under high pressure is very effective; short-term pressure works very well. In the long run, learning psychology shows us that it doesn't work. When the pressure is stopped, the effect is also gone. By continually applying pressure, you make the students rely on this pressure as a motivational crutch. Reward systems are inherently weak.

Studies have shown that when you reinforce positive behavior, the behavior tends to stop when you reduce the stimulus.[1] As teachers, we have process responsibility. We design a structure for meaningful change, plan implementation, and guide the process. This entails validation for successes and solace in difficult situations. Often, students need help in correctly evaluating their progress.

They tend to fail to see their progress altogether. The teacher then has to evaluate the situation in their stead (kind of like a substitute self). Sentences like, "This was very good. Do you see your own progress?" are helpful. For this to work, it is essential to direct the student's attention towards factual, easy to prove matters. (For example, when a skill was learned, which the student didn't have before.)

Many students require teachers to give them a professional evaluation, and that's okay. The danger is balancing communication too strongly towards criticism in class. In my opinion, it's most important to distinguish between a *professional assessment* and *personal judgment*. This may seem obvious, but it's tough to do in reality. I constantly ask myself, "Am I sure? Is this a true professional verdict? Or is it an expression of my own beliefs and preferences?"

A positive and productive student-teacher-relationship can offer many meaningful experiences - one of the most powerful is the feeling of *acceptance*. A teacher can demonstrate that the student is accepted as he or she is at the current moment. This has to be consistently done over an extended period of time to be effective. In turn, this experience can free a lot of energy for positive change. Students must feel that they are valuable even if they have not reached their full potential yet.

As humans, we use a lot of mental energy to continually evaluate our position regarding to other people, especially in hierarchies. This may be a heritage from earlier tribal societies, where the position in the tribe was crucial for survival in an evolutionary sense. Acceptance signals being *recognized* within the social hierarchy. To get the ball going and to demonstrate acceptance, I have had positive experiences with phrases like:

- "You are worth my best effort" (positive validation)
- "I understand your problem"
- "That I can imagine" (understanding)
- "This is a common problem" (normalization)
- "There are techniques to help with this" (prospect of success)
- "I will help you with everything I know" (support)
- "I can see that you have the resources you need" (resource-orientation)
- "I value how much you invest into this" (appreciation)

Teachers have a special status as experts; therefore, they must offer students *appreciation, hope,* and *activation of resources*. Saying the right things is meaningless, though, if it's not done in a good relationship.

Appreciation is by definition a fundamental attitude of acceptance, regardless of success or failure. In education, we tend to reward success and punish failure. Of course, we cannot escape the educational system altogether, but we can try to build a basis of relational engagement, respect, benevolence, appreciation, and interest independent of success. This is no romanticism - it's actually a very good strategy. In most cases, there is a reason, an obstacle, for failure. If we try to reduce these obstacles, we are much more likely to succeed.

When a student feels hopeless, depressed, or unsuccessful, acceptance can be a very meaningful resource for change. Appreciation allows the student to experience him or herself positively at this moment and to increase self-worth (a basic psychological need). This has a positive impact on motivation and the ability to push towards change.

Problems notwithstanding, students should be able to say the following sentences, "I'm likable. I'm basically okay. I'm worthy of someone's attention. My teachers trust my ability to push my level." If the student feels discouraged and frustrated, the teacher can demonstrate active involvement and interest and offer encouragement by saying:

- "It's understandable that you feel this way; this needs time." (acceptance)
- "I will not give up working with you on this matter." (secure attachment)
- "Even if this takes a while, we will do this together." (positive outlook)

We fulfill opposing roles when teaching. On the one hand, we need to offer support and guidance to students as a coach, and on the other hand, we are also responsible for giving grades. We must judge performance; we are referees and judges.

Even if this fact is not mentioned explicitly, it's safe to assume that students always know in the background of their minds that the teachers will evaluate them sooner or later. In my own career, this has led to some very difficult situations. The conflicting roles of "judge and coach together" can lead to *loyalty conflicts*.

I believe teachers need professional distance while being actively involved. Students should know that teachers care for their well-being, and not only during class. If teachers say, "I thought about what you said last time, and I wanted to tell you…", it shows the students that their contribution was meaningful and worthy of further reflection. It gives hope to the students that further progress is possible.

In psychotherapy, there have been numerous studies that show how hope is crucial. Hope and positive expectations are the best indicators for success.[2] I've seen it repeatedly; when a renowned expert comes to the school and offers encouragement or criticism, his or her position of authority alone helps boost self-esteem and confidence in students. It may very well be that the expert says *exactly* the same things as the teachers did before. Still, an outsider expert's status helps generate positive energy, which is very beneficial for overall success.

Hope is the valid expectation that things will get better. The impact of hope is even greater than the power of empathy or the special techniques used.[3] Many students have negative images of themselves deeply within - self-doubting beliefs such as, "I will never succeed; no one will accept me, or I'm not good enough," actually occur often.

It's important to promote a (reasonable) positive expectation. This reduces helplessness, pessimism, and overall depressiveness and leads to more engagement on the student's part. In turn, more engagement inforces self-efficacy and control. Hope is a sort of projection that is intensified by a high social status as an expert (a kind of halo-effect).

Hope is a positive attitude of resource-orientation, empathy and validation, and trust in technical advice.[4] The problem here is to find a suitable balance between instigating hope and raising unwarranted expectations. If expectations are too high, this will reinforce negative belief systems later because of *disappointment*. Disappointment can be avoided if, early on, the focus is directed towards the student's resources.

Activating resources doesn't simply happen - a conscious effort by the teacher is needed to balance problem-focused and resource-oriented interventions in class. As a teacher, I try to remind myself regularly of the student's strengths, skills, and qualities before entering a lesson. By doing so, I set my emotional tone to resource-orientation. It's like finding the TV channel I want. It's not zapping; it's a conscious effort.

Many factors influence success in teaching. Some very influential factors are typically not discussed in lessons; an attitude of *empathy* helps the student feel seen, accepted, and understood. It's rare to talk about prior experiences, emotions, and motives in class. But it's clear that these factors directly influence the lessons' outcomes - they affect our motivations, self-efficacy, and self-confidence.

Empathy is a crucial element in educational relationships - it's an important tool. In psychotherapy, its effectiveness is proven.[5] Empathy means to attempt to understand the other's inner emotions, motives, needs, and thoughts. Through empathy, we can get in touch with another person deeply. We can open emotional channels towards the other person and let ourselves be touched emotionally in turn.[6]

Empathy is more than just sharing something. It entails rational understanding as well. We must do both - try to see the other's perspective *rationally* and also understand their affective involvement *emotionally*. Empathy is based on human warmth; through empathy and validation, we can try to open up new avenues towards the student. These allow us to establish mutual trust. We can choose future interventions and techniques better.

Empathetic understanding is different from the every-day understanding of people. In every-day life, we understand others based on of our own emotions, fears, dreams, etc. As professionals, we must establish critical distance to our own inner states; our main task is *helping* the other, not *expressing* ourselves.

It is also necessary to gauge the intensity of the empathy you offer very accurately. In the beginning, when getting to know each other, it is a good approach to choose a relatively *superficial* level of empathy. This allows the other person to feel in control. You still don't know each other very well, and trust has to develop. Later, a deeper form of empathy can be very beneficial.

We can try to feel the impressions we receive from the student. We not only listen to the words said but are open to the inner reality behind those words. We attempt to sense the causes behind certain expressions and are sensitive to the associations they give us. We voice opinions and judgments guardedly. We engage in active listening.

Active listening means listening closely and attentively.[7] Many significant undercurrents in communication are not spoken out loud - close attention needs to be directed towards gestures, facial expressions, and inflections to decode them. When we do so, we can (gently) point out feelings and thoughts, which we *suppose* the other person has. This is an art; basically, it's conjecture. We might be right; we might be wrong. I'm always relieved when the reaction of the other person shows me that my assumptions were correct.

Empathy needs patience. Time pressure is one of the most common psychological stressors.[8] Just by being patient and giving the student space, we can already make things better.

Practitioner's Tip:
Sometimes, I feel overwhelmed. Between classes, students may approach me, telling me about some difficulty or a problem. It's good to be prepared. If you develop your professional communication skills, you have a shield to protect you. A few phrases and trained behaviors can give you the moments you need to collect yourself.

In "normal" life, we talk a lot of the time without giving it much thought. We ask questions; we listen. In a professional framework, our questions should gather new information from the student and help the other to better get in touch with themselves. You can say something like, "I would like to learn more about that" or "This seems to concern you."

I don't recommend the classic "How does that make you feel?" so much. It tends to bring the other person into a meta-state of evaluation. Often, it's more fruitful to try to stay with the emotion in question and not talk too much *about* it. After listening, the next step is to mirror and paraphrase what I believe in having understood to demonstrate empathy. This is crucial because it is this feedback, which allows the other person to really *feel understood*.

It makes the student feel my interest, my effort, and earnestness as a listener. Empty phrases like "I understand" should be avoided - they are too general. The other person doesn't feel valued if confronted merely with a cliché. It's much better to paraphrase something he or she said (mirroring).

Mirroring feedback can be worded as a question, "Am I understanding this correctly? You feel..." Or it can be a declarative sentence, "I understand that you are nervous about your professional future." The key ingredient is to make clear that we express what we *believe* in having understood.

Like in any relationship, getting to know each other is the most important part. I'm convinced that much of relationship building is done in informal settings. You meet in the hall, at the coffee machine, or in the cafeteria. You talk, and often the informality helps the other person to speak about difficult matters.

Some students prefer to feel emotional empathy. You can react to this by mirroring, "Listening to what you say, I feel..." Others are fond of a more rational mode, "It looks to me like you are putting yourself down here." In reality, you must be able to change very quickly between modes if needed.

Empathy is closely linked with validation, accepting the other person's reality is *true for this person* and *as valid at this moment*. Emotions, actions, and thoughts are rooted in personal experience - we can understand them through personal history. If you want to validate what someone just said, you can use this example, "If I had your experiences, I would most probably feel the same way." This is a sentence with many layers; it suggests to the other person that their feelings are comprehensible. It also makes it clear that they are not outlandish. The other person is not a freak - it's perfectly human to feel that way.

Being empathetic is attempting to *experience* the other's inner emotional world - it's sensing the other's thoughts and emotions. Validation is acknowledging the internal logic within his or her framework. Validation is understanding why he or she feels, thinks, and acts in a certain manner.

Validation does not mean that I subscribe to the other's worldview; it just means that I accept the other's perspective as rooted in individual experiences and thus as valid for him or her. I don't get into a discussion about whether it's right or wrong. This may seem trivial, but the method is actually quite challenging and can be very energy-consuming.

An attitude of positive validation gives the other person the feeling to be understood and comprehended. By accepting the other's view as a valid perspective, we reduce *antagonism*. The other person feels that we are on the same page. Why should we do that? Because until the other person feels understood, they will fight for being accepted and/or show resistance.

As in all of these things, a lot of flexibility is needed. If I'm too one-sided in my approach, only offering empathy and validation will give the other little incentive to change. At the right point, I need to switch to a more instructive, guiding strategy. Maybe even empathetic confrontation is needed. It's always a balancing act between empathy and validation on the one hand and orientation towards change on the other.

It's always a balancing act between empathy and validation on the one hand and orientation towards change on the other. Too much change orientation will result in resistance.
Too much empathy will lead to stagnation.

Too much change orientation will result in resistance, and too much empathy will lead to stagnation. Sometimes students come to me, asking for a more *directional* approach in my teaching. I tend to see this as a positive reaction to my approach - it shows a dose of dissonance in the interaction. Dissonance can be very constructive because differences become apparent. It also shows that the relational basis is good enough for this type of criticism. A success!

There are two ways to deal with this dissonance. First, I can change my interaction strategy, and second, I can interpret this statement as a coping strategy. It can be that students feel strange when in an empathetic educational relationship. Maybe they are not used to that, or perhaps it makes them feel insecure. I like to ask, "Why do you think you need more guidance?"

Accepting the other person is a great gift. Acceptance is recognizing the other person as valuable by him or herself. However, it does not mean refraining from criticism; criticism and guidance are necessary for change.

Acceptance doesn't necessarily mean that I must like the other person — it is not based on sympathy; it's a professional attitude. It's our ability to recognize a person's value, even if this person shows behavior that we perceive as different or problematic. With empathy and acceptance, we actively search for background knowledge and try to understand why a student thinks or behaves in a particular manner. When I see that there are experiences behind certain behaviors, it's easier for me to be honestly empathetic.

For example, sometimes it's hard for me to accept criticism from students; I feel that they act quite selfishly from time to time. They tend to offer harsh judgment towards others (like me), the school, other teachers, etc., failing to see that all these people are individuals with emotions like themselves. Of course, there is room for criticism, but it's important to recognize that people at work (for the most part) try very hard to make studying a good experience for the students.

This reaction to criticism is (of course) projection on my part. I share this example because I need a mentalizing effort to bring down the emotional temperature within myself at that moment. My feelings of being wrongly accused have nothing to do with the situation itself. Acceptance of the other person means very specifically that I do not voice my negative emotions in this situation. I can do so later with my friends or colleagues. I can do that in therapy (if I wish), but the educational relationship itself is not the right place to do that.

In short, what we need in education is the functional management of the teacher-student-relationship. We need to be able to switch communication modes quickly, assuming many roles, allowing for a high grade of flexibility when facing different individual situations and conditions. Empathy is understanding, validation is comprehension, and acceptance means refraining from judgment. As a rule of thumb, a good progression is showing empathy and offering validation, and only *then*, offer advice (change orientation).

Important points to remember

✓ Teachers have a process responsibility and a special status as experts.

✓ Saying the right things is meaningless if it's not done in a good relationship. Students should know that teachers care for their well-being.

✓ Empathy is a crucial element in educational relationships. Empathy is to attempt to understand the other's inner emotions, motives, needs, and thoughts.

✓ Empathy is closely linked with validation. Validation means accepting the other person's reality as true for this person and as valid at this moment.

✓ Too much change orientation will result in resistance. Too much empathy will lead to stagnation. Instead, show empathy, offer validation, and then offer advice (change orientation).

Chapter references

1   An interesting study in this regard: Warneken, Felix, Tomasello, Michael (2008): "Extrinsic Rewards undermine Altruistic Tendencies in 20-Month-Olds."*Developmental Psychology*, 44 (6), 1785-1788.

2   See Swift J.K. & Derthick A.O. (2013): "Increasing hope by addressing client's outcome expectancies." *Psychotherapy*, 50, 284–287.

3   As shown for psychotherapy in a study by Martin D.J., Garske J.P. & Davis M.K. (2000): "Relation of the therapeutic alliance with outcome and other variables: A meta-analytic review." Journal of Consulting and Clinical Psychology, 68, 438–450.

4   For more information, see Messer S.B. & Wampold B.E. (2002): "Let's face facts: Common factors are more potent than specific therapy ingredients."*American Psychological Association*, 9, 21–25.

5   See Vyskocilova J., Prasko J. & Slepecky M. (2011): "Empathy in cognitive behavioral therapy and supervision." *Activitas Nervosa Superior Redivia*, 53, 72–83.

6   For more on this, please refer to Elliot R., Bohart A.C., Watson J.C. & Greenberg L.S. (2011): "Empathy." *Psychotherapy: Theory, Research, Practice, Training*, 48, 43–49.

7   *Active listening* is used here in the meaning as purported by Carl Rogers. There is an interesting study on attachment-style and the efficacy of active listening: Castro, Dotan R., Kluger, Avraham N., Itzchakov, Guy (2016): "Does avoidance-attachment style attenuate the benefits of being listened to?" *European Journal of Social Psychology*, 46, 6.

8   See Svenson, Ola, Maule, A. John (1993): *Time Pressure and Stress in Human Judgment and Decision Making*. New York: Springer US.

Chapter 20
General Dynamics:
Phases, Interpersonal Competences, and Structure

Relationships are shaped through communication; they are dynamic and subject to change. Relationships have different phases; they often follow a sequence. Inevitably, they also end sooner or later. (This is a concept I still find difficult to accept).[1]

For group relationships, Tuckman (as early as 1965) formulated four distinctive stages. He named them forming, storming, norming, and performing. (I will use them here as an example of how relationships can develop.)

The *forming* phase is characterized by the group members being on their best behavior but relatively uninformed about each other and their tasks. This phase focuses on getting to know each other and becoming familiar. The next, the *storming* phase, is centered on developing a relationship - it's about setting the internal hierarchy and starting to trust each other professionally. (Interestingly, some teams never mature past this stage).

If successful, storming leads to the next phase, *norming* - a shift of attention towards a common goal. This entails taking responsibility for the overall outcome and working out controversies in a constructive manner. When norms and goals are clear, the group can perform (*performing* stage). Most benefits are achieved during this stage. If team membership changes, the cycle is repeated until the new members are incorporated into the existing social structure.

That's the sequence, according to Tuckman (in a nutshell). Tuckman added another phase later, *adjourning*, which occurs when the team breaks up and comes to grips with ending the collaboration. Adjourning can be quite emotional.

In teaching, we deal with groups or have one-to-one settings. I think that even in one-to-one educational relationships, this model can be helpful. In the beginning, we need to build an effective connection (that would be *forming*). We must clarify our roles and define goals (*norming*).

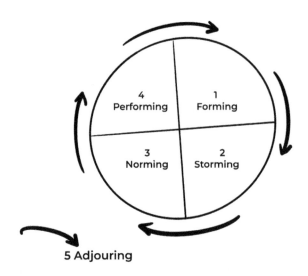

Phases of group development according to Tuckman (1965).

In my experience, the start of an educational relationship is a period of mixed feelings. Students enter an institution of learning (school, college, university) and come into a new environment. They must first get their bearings, establish themselves within their groups, and their relationship with the teachers. This phase can be full of excitement but also intense anxiety. Social acceptance, worthiness, and insecurity are difficult topics to grapple with.

Entering the *performing* stage, we need to first analyze the need for change, the necessity to learn new skills, or alter behavior and thought patterns. Then we can go about it. When performing is done, *adjourning* follows. I often see that a teaching process simply ends by default because the school year ends or exams. That's a missed opportunity!

Endings can be powerful for further motivation. Taking process responsibility seriously, we, as teachers, must name successes as such. Rituals help in this regard.

For example, a graduation ceremony can function as a "rite of passage," a symbolic end of a distinct phase in the students' lives.[2]

When a secure relationship is offered, I'm often surprised how much relief the quality of the realtionship in itself already offers. Seeing that someone is earnestly interested in helping already makes change easier.

Often, students are scared they won't be accepted or taken seriously. If they have problems, they are ashamed to address them. They often think problems are solely their fault, and they have to work them out alone. They sometimes perceive problems as weaknesses to be purged. In most cases, they are not used to opening up to a teacher about personal topics, their needs, or burdens.

In the beginning, unburdening and building trust are the most critical elements. A positive, affective atmosphere must be established, and an optimistic vision of the future must be generated and resources activated.

Trust is built through empathy, validation, and acceptance. The students' experiences are accepted as valid from their perspective, so be careful with value judgments. Resistance can occur when the interaction style is too confrontational. Rather than pushing for self-disclosure, the teacher's *expertise* should be *demonstrated* and *acceptance offered*. Over time, this will lead to an atmosphere that allows the students to open up. In the course of this, benevolent feedback can be encouraged.

According to a study by Fiske et al., humans (like all social animals) must quiclkly distinguish if a person we meet is friendly towards us or not.[3] It seems like there are two universal dimensions to this: social *warmth* and *competence*. Is the person friendly? Can the person act on his or her intentions? Very quickly, we assess where we stand in relation to the other person.

We judge based on evaluation of cues - clothing style, gestures, and vocal tone are all cues. The interpretation of these cues proves to be surprisingly accurate. Far from being merely superficial, outside cues offer valuable information about the other. Our personality manifest in many ways in our outward appearance.[4]

We tend to see people we experience as warm and competent as potential *friends* and *allies* - we have positive emotions towards them. People we experience as neither warm nor competent receive a negative emotional response; therefore, it is crucial be warm and competent to establish good relationships.

In therapy, the quality of the relationship predicts success.[5] I'm convinced it is the same in teaching, but even if teachers do everything right and offer the best relationship to the student, failure is still possible. It's possible that the student does not develop trust.[6]

Trust is either given or not given. We form our judgment, our perception of another person, very fast. Therefore, I suggest asking students directly after a few interactions, "Do you feel that you have come to the right place? Are you happy?" If not, it's better to change approaches immediately. If the relationship simply doesn't work, I recommend changing teachers quickly. To be stuck in an unfruitful educational relationship is no fun for all parties involved.

I might decide to stop working with an individual student if there are demonstrably no positive results, if the student does not participate enough (despite strong efforts by the teacher), or if there's destructive or aggressive behavior. And I might earnestly feel as a teacher that I'm not the right teacher for this person.

That's okay. If the teacher decides to end lessons prematurely, the detachment should follow the same rules as under normal circumstances. Generally, ending the relationship should be as *cooperative* as the relationship itself.

When the starting phases (*forming* and *storming*) are over, we have gotten to know each other and have hopefully developed trust. Now it's time to reset the course (*norming* and *performing*). A fresh look at the student and their judgments and behaviors is needed; this can be a more *critical* look. As a teacher, I must offer more structure and guidance in this phase. I must point out where I see that change is needed. The student might not experience me as supportive and understanding as before.

This can put a strain on the relationship. Maybe, the student has to tackle difficult emotions, like anxiety, stress, embarrassment, or loneliness. It's tricky territory. Teachers have to look out for a drop in motivation, lack of participation, or general discontent in the students. If you see that motivation suddenly drops or that students don't invest as much as before, go back to validation and acceptance.

If this phase is successful, this is the point where the most progress is made. Don't be afraid to go back and forth between the opposing poles of (1) pushing for progress (change) and (2) offering acceptance a few times. Be open and try to feel what the student needs most at this moment.

Toward the end of an educational relationship, students should be able to work autonomously. I like to say that as teachers, we work towards making ourselves redundant. Our goal is that students won't need us any longer. Toward the end, we give less structuring assistance and guide less - we can consciously take a step back.

We should not offer so much reassurance at this point; instead, we can ask for the student's self-assessment. By doing so, the student can learn to develop a balanced judgment of their achievements. The student can learn to praise him- or herself without needing the teacher's approval.

However, this should not be done too early in the process. If you do it too early, it will just come off as a *mind game*. Don't you hate it when you go to a performance review, and your boss opens the interview by asking you, "So, what do YOU think about your performance?" I always hated that! So, take your time posing these questions. Make sure that the relationship is sound before guiding the student toward self-assessment. It must be clear that you aren't trying to put them on the spot.

At the very end of an educational relationship, there is the process of detachment.[7] (Or what Tuckman calls *adjourning*.) Since academic relationships have personal and professional aspects, this is often a difficult process. Many times, one party (or the other) instigates conflict to make the pain of separation more bearable. Usually, this looks like the better option. Believe me; it's not. An emotional volcano outbreak is like ripping off a band-aid - short but intensely painful. There can be deep emotional scars from this.

Ending a relationship is momentous - it needs special care. It's not only that we got used to each other, but we also built an *affective relationship*. Teacher and student both have to let go of a meaningful connection upon leaving, especially when the academic relationship was successful. It's a two-sided relationship. The teacher has offered not only knowledge but also reassurance, acceptance, and empathy in the formative phases of the student's development. Likewise, students can become very important to teachers. It's expected that the teacher will be affected emotionally by the end of the educational relationship, too.

I recommend addressing the end of the educational relationship early. It's important for all sides to know (and learn to accept) that it will run its course and then end. This can be emotionally challenging, and when there aren't many lessons left, it's good to ask, "How do you feel about that?" I suggest giving detachment enough room at the end of the educational process.[8] Rituals (like giving gifts or mementos) can also help navigate this difficult territory.

The ending phase raises the opportunity to look back together and give each other valuable feedback. Within limits, I encourage to openly say, "I really liked working with you, and I'm very happy about what you have achieved." To make this transition easier, it's possible to offer less frequent lessons until they are not longer needed (for reassurance). A well-managed ending can be a parting gift for both sides; it can help keep a good memory of the whole relationship. We tend to evaluate processes based on the feeling we have at the end of them.[9]

Contrary to psychotherapy, teachers and students can become friends when the educational relationship is over. Even so, this is a big shift. The character of the relationship changes and this must be clear to all parties involved.

Now we know about typical phases.

And the next question is, "Precisely, how do we navigate them?" This must be achieved through communication. The way we guide communication is the practical application of the fundamentals outlined above. We must put the fundamentals into practice. Basically, it's the ability to see others, understand them, speak and listen to them, and help them solve their problems. Let's call those interpersonal *competencies* of the teacher.[10]

Teaching is an art because there are no strict recipes for success. The same is true for communication. Many approaches are opposed to each other — and can be equally good. At the beginning of a teaching career, it's hard to know precisely when to ask a follow-up question, confront empathetically, offer validation, summarize, listen actively, or guide the discussion.

Psychotherapy has the same problem. A valid and established theory of communication applicable for all people and all situations does not exist. In varying situations, different people profit from different approaches. Which techniques to be used can only be answered by the other person's personality - look at his or her needs. At certain times, different approaches can be suitable. Generally, it's good to aim your communication at strengthening the educational relationship, and always keep in mind that you're in an *alliance* with the student. Find coherence in goals and techniques and form an affective bond (see Bordin 1979).

Practitioner's Tip:
I very much recommend recording lessons on video. It's painful, I admit, but in my experience, there is nothing more helpful. Observational learning always has more impact than reading a book. Seeing yourself on screen makes you immediately aware of how you appear to others. You can see more clearly how students react to you. To make this even more fruitful, I suggest watching these videos with others (in a supervision-type setting).

Coherence in goals and techniques brings me to the next point - lessons should have a clear and reliable *structure*. This structure supports reaching the goals you set together. It also offers orientation. Through structure, the student already knows what the goals are, which approaches will be used, what is asked of them, and which successes were already achieved.

In the sense of observational or model-learning, structuring the lessons is a teaching in itself. It shows the student how to approach a topic, goal-oriented and structured. A possible structure might look like this:

- **A greeting, asking if something special has happened:**
  "How are you?" sounds trivial but is expected by students. To further

express that I care, I often immediately follow up with something I remember from the last meeting like, "How did the test go?" (if there was a test at school) or "Did your parents like your performance?" (if there was a performance).

- **Asking for homework and successes:**

   "How did you manage with...? What went well? What was difficult?" Use the information you receive for further questions. You can go quite deep into matters quickly this way. Here, some technical rituals can occur (in music, for example, *scales* or *etudes*).

- **Establishing a goal for development:**

   "Would you like to look deeper into...? How would you like to go about it?" At this point, new things can be worked on, and homework can be given.

- **Interventions:**

   According to the students' needs, you follow their lead and support the progress through interventions - providing technical advice, offering psychological support, talking about stress or anxiety, etc.

- **Summary and feedback:**

   "How did you feel in today's lesson? Do you feel like we're on the right track? Your work today was excellent; thank you for your hard work!" I find it very important to end lessons on a positive note and strengthen the relationship. The closing statement should be affirmative and (if possible) enjoyable, with positive emotions (shared laughter, humor).

These are the phases, interpersonal competencies, and structuring elements I would like to recommend. The next chapter will focus on communication itself.

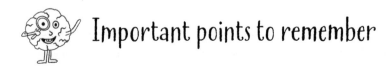

Important points to remember

✓ Relationships have different phases, a sequence. They are dynamic.

✓ The start of an educational relationship is a period of mixed feelings. Social acceptance, worthiness, and insecurity are difficult topics to grapple with.

✓ Trust is built through empathy, validation, and acceptance.

✓ The quality of the relationship predicts success in teaching. To be seen as warm and competent is crucial for establishing good relationships.

✓ Ending a relationship is momentous; it needs special care.

✓ Lessons should have a clear and reliable structure. In the sense of observational or model-learning, structuring the lessons is a teaching in itself.

Chapter references

1   A very helpful form in this regard was the sequence of group development as formulated by Bruce Tuckman. It can be found here: Tuckman, Bruce W. (1965): "Developmental Sequence in Small Groups." Psychological Bulletin, 63 (6), 384-399.

2   Also, this can mitigate the (painful) emotions of ending a long-lasting educational relationship.

3   See Fisk, Susa T., Cuddy, Amy J.C., Glick, Peter (2007): "Universal dimensions of social cognition: warmth and competence." *TRENDS in Cognitive Sciences*, 11 (2).

4   Naumann, laura P., Vazire, Simine, Rentfrow, Peter J., Gosling, Samuel D. (2009): "Personality Judgments Based on Physical Appearance."*Pers Soc Psychol Bull*, 35; 1661.

5   See Martin et al., (2000).

6   Studies show that we decide within fractions of seconds whether someone is worthy of our trust or not. See Wampold B.E. & Budge S.L. (2012): "The relationship – and its relationship to common and specific factors of psychotherapy." *Society of Counseling Psychology*, 40, 601–623.

7   For more information, see Zimmer D. (2000): "Therapiebeendigung – Ideen aus einer kognitiv-behavioralen Perspektive."Verhaltenstherapie und Verhaltensmedizin, 21(4), 469-480.

8   For psychotherapy, there is a lot of valuable information about this topic. For example, Ocha E. & Muran J.C. (2008): "A relational take on termination in cognitive-behavioral therapy." W.T. O'Donohue & M.A. Cucciare (Eds.): *Terminating Psychotherapy*. New York: Routledge.

9   In psychology, this is called the *peak-end rule*. See Kemp, Simon, Burt, Christopher D. B., Furneaux, Laura (2008): "A test oft he peak-end rule with extended autobiographical events." *Memory & Cognition*, 36 (1) 132-138.

10   Interpersonal competencies can make difficult processes much easier: Anderson T., Ogles B.M., Patterson C.L., Lambert M.J., Vermeersch D.A. (2009): "Therapist effects: Facilitative interpersonal skills as a predictor of therapist success." *Journal of Clinical Psychology*, 65, 755–768.

Chapter 21

"What You See Is What You Get": Verbal & Non-verbal Communication, Preparation, and Guided Exploration

Teaching is a structured process with different phases; communication is at its center. Communication is not only about the words you choose; it's also how you modulate your voice, how you stress certain words, the facial expressions you have, and how you behave overall.

I gathered together a "tool kit" for my own use, and I would like to share it here with you. I recommend using these techniques as *interventions*. They are best for one-to-one settings. This can be a counseling session or an informal talk in the hallway. It's not always the big formal sessions that have the greatest impact - a short exchange can be immensely beneficial. Be careful in groups because you don't want to expose a person and their problems in front of others.

As teachers, we are no robots - we have emotions. We need mental hygiene, have to become aware of our projections, and must balance our communication. First and foremost, a balanced communication and professionalism in the way we use it.

We communicate all the time. In a professional setting, we must be alert to how we communicate and how we talk and behave to others. Verbal and non-verbal communication greatly influences whether students see teachers as competent, likeable and worthy of trust.

Students assess teachers based on cues. If you modulate the cues you give, you can influence the result. Here a few key elements.[1]

We communicate all the time: Students assess teachers based on cues.
Teachers need to be very aware of the cues they give.

Non-verbal:

- Upright posture (shows interest and being engaged)
- Relatively open arms and little movement with the legs
- Congruence in body-language (mirroring)
- Eye contact and gestures
- Showing attentiveness and interest by nodding or smiling

The words we choose influence our communication's success, and the complexity of how we speak also has a great impact. I know that I'm prone to using too many long-winded sentences. I try my best to make it shorter and more on the point, and since I started doing this, I've realized that my communication improved. I recommend avoiding science lingo whenever possible (because it's a distancing behavior).

Verbal style:

- Sympathetic
- Calm
- Warm
- Positive
- Interested

It's important not to rush things. Give students time to think. Especially in the beginning, young teachers tend to ask something and then answer their own questions. They can not bear silence stretching out. I recommend counting from one to five inside your head. This gives your mind something to do and makes waiting easier.

When asking questions, it is helpful to distinguish between *open* and *closed* ones. Closed questions are simply answered by yes or no. They are very structured, and you don't get much additional information. You can use them when you want quick, precise information about something. For example, "Did you find the address easily?"

Closed questions lead to a relatively *passive* attitude. Often, after a yes or no, nothing much happens. This is why it's essential to also use *explorative* questions: how, why, when, and what. By thinking about these questions, the student must come up with answers by themselves. A simple yes or no is not enough. This boosts active interaction and leads to self-exploration. To answer these questions, the student has to reflect before responding.

I recommend not falling into interrogation-mode, especially when getting to know each other. Assume that the student is nervous - don't make him or her feel as if under cross-examination. Instead, ask opening questions without too much eye-contact (maybe while closing the window or something like that). This will give the student some space.

Many people tend to have deficit orientation. As the old cliche goes, they see the glass as half-empty. This is actually good in an evolutionary sense. Our brain is geared towards keeping us alive, not towards helping us leading blissful lives. The brain normally tries to distinguish possible threats and to avoid them; therefore, it tends to have a rather bleak outlook on the world, always trying to detect the next danger around the corner.

Practitioner's Tip:
The good news is you can change the way you think through the language you use (it's the old NLP paradigm[2]). When talking with students, try to avoid generalizations: "I'm always criticized", "I never manage to…". Instead, use sometimes, often, etc. For example, if a student says, "I'm always criticized," you can counter with, "I understand that you're often criticized; when do you get praised?" Or if they say, "I never manage to…", you can reply with, "Sometimes you don't get around to…, but is there a time when you did manage?"

When a student speaks of an unattainable goal, "I can't play Tchaikovsky concerto," you can react with "not yet". For example, "So, you aren't able to play it yet?" In a very subtle way, this opens up the possibility of reaching that goal in the student's mind.

Many students tend to polarize the language they use and to draw catastrophic images when assessing themselves. "That was unbearable" or "I was mortally afraid." You can counter by using a more realistic and neutral language. "You see great difficulties in this" or "You've had great anxiety." Toning it down helps the other to see problems more realistically and opens up avenues for change. If everything is hopeless, there is really no need for development.

As in many aspects of life, preparation is key. Before (important) interactions, teachers should remember and consult their notes. It's good to know what the topic previously was, if there was some sort of homework, or how to proceed from here.

On the relationship-based level, it's helpful to remember some individual traits of the other person. If possible, take a few moments to get into the mode of the student you're interacting with. Ask yourself:

- How should I shape the relationship (based on the other's needs)?
- Which feelings do I have, and how can I best cope with them?
- How can I activate the other's resources best?
- Which approaches and techniques have previously worked best with this person?
- Which traps would I like to avoid?

In interactions, you can use your empathy for a variety of purposes.[3] In psychotherapy, there is quite a lot of literature on this. The most important concepts are:

- **Empathetic *understanding*:**
  This basic form of empathy is reflecting back. You tell the other person what you think you understood (I sense anger and helplessness in the way you talk. Is that how you feel?)
- **Empathetic *affirmation*:**
  What you say empathetically should give the other person the perception that it's okay to think and feel how he or she does (Of course, this thought makes you sad; that's perfectly understandable).
- **Empathetic *deepening*:**
  Here, you try to make an emotional experience deeper and broader (This

feels like you're all alone in the world and no one is interested in you, right?).

- **Empathetic *exploration*:**

  This kind of empathy aims to help the other focus the attention on some specific aspects. We never see a situation in its totality; sometimes, we need someone to help us. You can gently point out factors that were avoided or ignored before. (At this moment, you're very sad and lonely. Maybe there are other thoughts and feelings as well?)

- **Empathetic *conjecture*:**

  In this technique, you express your own experience when listening. This allows the other person to explore their (hidden) thoughts and feelings. (When you told me about your sadness, I felt a constricting sense of anxiety, as if all hope was lost.") The other person can then build on top of that. It makes talking about difficult topics easier if someone builds you a bridge.

In order to be truly empathetic, you must aim to free yourself of your own thoughts, motives, goals, wishes, and emotions. Of course, that's impossible, but the point is to try to establish *some* distance. I often realize that some statements make me angry — not because they are so infuriating, but because they touch some experiences I had in *my* life. But my life is not the topic at hand. It's about opening up towards the other. Therefore, the first step is to aimlessly experience what the other person says without an agenda. Be resonant emotionally. Your rationality then will offer further insight.

Helpful questions to pose to yourself are:

- Which messages do I get from the other person?
- What is he /she feeling or thinking right now?
- Which expectations, needs, or motives are relevant for the other now?
- How does he/she likely perceive the current situation?
- How do I react emotionally to the tone of voice, gestures, and facial expressions?

I firmly believe that to understand other people deeply, you must know your own experiences well. This is necessary because we address the emotional inside world of others through our own representations of emotions.[4] If I know my own anxieties, egoism, envy, loneliness, sympathies, etc., I can react better when I see these traits in other people.[5]

Empathy and validation go together. The greatest gift we have for other people is our undivided attention. Through facial expressions, gestures, and single words, we demonstrate that we are listening (nodding, signaling agreement by using yes, aha, or okay). This is best combined with accurate reflection (empathy) on the same level. You mirror what the other person said without offering judgment. You can say something like, "I understand that you feel...(fill in what the other said)." On top of that, you can express how you perceive the other person during this talk. "The way you talk about this, I feel that you're not only sad, but maybe also disappointed? Even a bit bitter?"

It's also vital to demonstrate that you've understood the other person's main experiences and that their problems are understandable. "Keeping in mind your experiences, it's absolutely understandable that you are afraid of criticism/playing in public, etc." This validation is based on past experiences. A second approach is to use the current context for validation. Reflect on the other person's appraisal, "If you assess the situation like this, I can totally understand how you feel and why you acted in the manner you did." or "In this situation, your emotions were so strong, you couldn't act differently, right?"

A third approach is normative validation - when the other person's behavior is positively accepted. "That you became angry when your best friend ridiculed you in front of others is absolutely okay. It's important for your friend to understand that you were hurt." The validation approach may seem low-key at first, but it can yield great successes. By experiencing validation from a significant other, a person can learn to accept them with empathy. It's like giving license to a new behavior.[6]

You can learn sentences, gestures, and behaviors that *express* empathy, but mental hygiene is needed. It will remain an empty technique if it's not carried out by true compassion. First, you need self-compassion to be able to offer it to others. Learn to treat yourself with compassion, understanding, and with a supportive attitude.[7]

One way to show compassion to another is by being interested. Attentive and active listening signals show a willingness to participate and emotional commitment. It consists of the following traits:

- Confirming behaviors (nodding, smiling, aha, mmh)
- Reflective listening (periodic eye contact, listening posture)
- Frequent summarizing of the most important points
- Clarifying questions (Do I understand correctly...?)

In active listening, you honestly try to understand the other person and demonstrate this by paraphrasing. The developing exchange in and of itself builds trust immediately. Additionally, paraphrasing helps tremendously in understanding the other person. By re-formulating something you heard from the other person in your own words, you gain new insights. Often, clarifying questions and paraphrasing help to get deeper into matters. If I misunderstood, the other person could easily correct me without having to fear retribution.

Practitioner's Tip — important behaviors to display:
- *Eye contact. By holding (short) eye contact regularly, you signal connection, understanding, and interest.*
- *Posture. Leaning towards the other person with open arms.*
- *Gestures and speech melody. A warm, friendly cadence, confirming gestures, showing agreement through smiling and nodding.*
- *"Receipt reactions." You can say, "Okay, Obviously, Really, I understand, and Yes" (make sure to alternate between them).*
- *Modulate stops. If the other person stops in the middle of saying something, you can repeat the last words and try to empathize to get things going again.*

It is difficult to express *exactly* what we feel, what moves us, and how we think. The techniques of active and reflective listening can help, and simply repeating a sentence can be a powerful tool. Paraphrasing builds trust to avoid misunderstanding. It also allows steering the discussion by giving structure to it. By paraphrasing, we can slow down someone who is talking rapidly and animatedly.

The impact is even greater when combined with verbalizing emotional experiences. You can paraphrase the content of a sentence and then add an emotional value statement like, "Solving your problems at school seems most important to you; you seem anxious about it. On the other hand, I have the feeling you're also angry about it?"

Reflective listening is not about interpretation or exploring things - that comes later. We try to follow the other person and make sure we understand correctly. We are thus a *resonating surface* and offer free space and control over the way the interaction goes.

Summarizing is the logical consequence of reflective listening - its main aim is to show that you have listened and understood. The other person feels validated just through this alone. He or she can then clarify things further and elaborate if needed.

Clarifying questions help to be more concrete, specific, and precise. Students encountering difficult life situations often offer stereotypical, catastrophic, imprecise, and one-sided views on their experiences. Avoidance behaviors make matters worse in this regard. If I avoid something, I don't analyze it thoroughly. Therefore, friendly but determined clarification helps the other person see themselves more clearly.

For example, if a student says, "That was unbearable!" you can ask, "What precisely did you think now? What exactly was unbearable?" If they say, "I will never manage," you can clarify with, "What's keeping you from doing so?" or "What are you aiming for precisely?"

When clarifying, it's important to ask only *one* question. Multiple questions tend to go unanswered (only the last question receives the attention). Multiple questions feel like cross-examination (Did you feel nervous? Did you have a panic attack? Were you angry, insecure, and unable to act?). They overwhelm. It's better to ask only one thing.

Asking questions goes *contrary* to avoidance behavior. Questions force us to confront something; therefore, it can come across confrontational. This can be uncomfortable for the other person. As a strategy, you can use questions to follow up on a thought process that the other seeks to avoid. Many students have strong anxieties concerning their professional future. By asking qualifying questions, I can try to help them see the resources they have; maybe they just weren't able to see them by themselves.

It's hard for students to open up on problematic and stressful experiences, thoughts, emotions, and behaviors, especially at the beginning of an educational relationship. This avoidance is often rooted in embarrassment, fear of criticism, shame, or lack of trust in the teacher.

It can help to openly address the problem we assume the other person has, especially if the issue at hand is something frequently encountered like exam anxiety or *stage fright*. Sometimes, openly expressing what the problem is may be a bridge too far for the other person, and it can be very liberating to hear another person say it. It's normalizing the problem, and normalizing reduces pressure. If I experience my problems as "not so outlandish" and "can be addressed," this already helps me to see myself as *basically okay*.

Maybe all of this feels too psychological for you.

Maybe you're thinking, "What else should I do? I'm a teacher, after all! My job is to teach, not offer therapy." That's absolutely true. In education, we generally focus a lot on knowledge, and that's fine. The great difficulty is self-efficacy (see Bandura 1982).

For our overall success in life, it's not so important how much knowledge and how many skills we have in total. The real clinch is, *can we act on it under pressure?* Often, thought patterns we gained through life keep us from performing on the level we actually could perform on.

I believe it's crucial to actively change unuseful thought patterns, especially when detrimental and dysfunctional. In a cooperative relationship, teachers will not manage to change thought patterns by confronting students *head-on*. The rational, discursive approach of "Let's talk about it" and "I'll try to make you change your mind" will not work. Unfortunately, most teachers try this path. They are explicit, trying the route through rational understanding. Mostly to no avail.

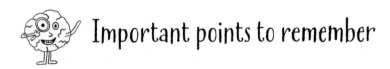

Important points to remember

✓ Balanced communication, first and foremost: Professionalism in the way we use our communication.

✓ By experiencing validation from a significant other, a person can learn to treat them with empathy.

✓ In active listening, you honestly try to understand the other person, demonstrated by paraphrasing.

Chapter references

1   This is taken from Merten J. (2001): *Beziehungsregulation in der Psychotherapie. Maladaptive Beziehungsmuster und der therapeutische Prozess.* Stuttgart: Kohlhammer.

2   If you're interested in NLP, I recommend reading Bodenhamer, Bob G., Hall, Michael L. (1999): *The User's Manual For The Brain.* Carmarthen: Crown House Publishing.

3   The reference here is Bischkopf J. (2013): *Emotionsfokussierte Therapie.* Göttingen: Hogrefe.

4   This process is called secondary representation. See Fonagy, Peter, Target, Mary (2002): "Neubewertung der Entwicklung der Affektregulation vor dem Hintergrund von Winnicotts Konzept des »falschen Selbst«." *Psyche-Z Psychoanal*, 56, 839–862.

5   See Thich Nhat Hanh's foreword in Weare, Katherine, Hanh, Thich Nhat (2017): *Happy teachers change the world. A guide for cultivating mindfulness in education.* Berkeley: Parallax Press.

6   There is a whole branch of therapy called compassion-focused therapy based on this paradigm. See Gilbert, Paul (2010): "An Introduction to Compassion Focused Therapy in Cognitive Behavior Therapy." *International Journal of Cognitive Therapy*, 3 (2), 97-112.

7   See Hwang, Yoon-Suk, Medvedev, Oleg N., Krägeloh, Chris, Hand, Kirstine, Noh, 1&Jae-Eun, Singh, Nirbhay N. (2019): "The Role of Dispositional Mindfulness and Self-compassion in Educator Stress," *Mindfulness*, 10:1692–1702

Chapter 22

Leadership, Reinforcement, and Metacommunication

Think about leadership. Leadership doesn't necessarily mean that you have to be in front. You can guide a process by following, asking clarifying questions, or offering summaries. Rather than providing ready-made solutions, you can help others find individual solutions. This technique is called *guided exploration.*

For example, telling a student with exam anxiety directly and explicitly that his avoidance strategy makes his misery worse will not be helpful. In addition to being miserable, he will also feel shame. It's better to ask questions concerning possible solutions, strategies, and past experiences. In turn, this helps the student to correct perceptions and question them. It's an implicit process.

In teaching, you must provide a balance. On the one hand, it is our job to offer advice, technical help, and perspectives for change. On the other hand, we must avoid making the students dependent on us. When we only provide solutions, the students won't learn to be self-reliant. Over time, we must enable them to find answers by themselves, so they don't need us. That's the reason why I find scientific thinking so important. Trial and error is a great strategy, and even better is a culture of skepticism, aimed conjecture, formulating a hypothesis, and testing it.

Teaching should have the form of a dialogue characterized by respect, empathy, and dignity. It aims to show discrepancies by posing well-aimed questions. The effect we want is *cognitive restructuring.*

Four approaches are possible here:

- **Choose to be *empirical*:**
  "What's the likelihood that your anxiety is warranted? Which evidence is there that your anxieties are right?"
- **Argue *logically*:**
  "If your teacher doesn't like you, why would they then offer you this chance to perform?"
- **Use a *functional* argument (arguing usefulness):**
  "If your goal is to perform better, how helpful is it when you thought that no one likes your performances?"
- **Argue *normatively*, search for possible discrepancies in values:**
  "If being perfect in all areas of life is so important to you, do you think that all people should have this standard, too?"

A mistake easily made in dialogue is not giving the other person enough room to speak about their fears. Give it enough space. If you push back too soon, you will get *resistance*. The other person then feels hindered and maybe even boxed in. It may seem like I haven't really made an effort to understand, or it may look like I jumped immediately to offering ready-made solutions instead of listening.

An important part of personal growth (and learning in general) is to *confront* problematic emotions. Teacher-student interactions too often rely on rational aspects of learning: Skills, knowledge, and technique. Too seldom, deeper emotions like shame, guilt, loneliness, sadness, anxiety, helplessness, etc., are brought up. Obviously, these emotions are very delicate. They are fundamental to overall educational success because they touch upon our self-image, motivations, and our aspirations.

What can we do as teachers?

Emotions are stimulated through our sensual experiences. By adjusting your choice of words, you can guide the other person toward exploring problematic situations.[1] Mirroring the other's words works very well. Trying to avoid difficult emotions is understandable and all too human. Unfortunately, avoidance tends to make matters worse.

A typical behavior leading to avoidance is psychological distancing. If you talk about events in the far future, there is a lot of distance from the current situation. This distance facilitates avoidance, but problems should be looked at in their actual concern in the present.

Talking in the abstract (using imprecise terms) also helps to build distance. To label something rather abstractly "a difficult encounter" is much easier than getting into the concrete nitty-gritty of "who said/did/experienced what? And why?"

Rationalization is another tool that allows for distancing difficult emotions. By reflecting on other people's motives, developing models of their behavior, or engaging in building fancy constructs, I can create a large gap between the situation and how it makes me feel.

Another way is to address emotions and not to give them enough space. Avoidance may feel like the easy way; it's not. The way you talk as a teacher can have a significant impact in this regard. It can help the other person have the courage to look deeper into problems and subsequently address them.

Teachers are guides; they help students find their path in unknown territory. The key to success lies in using the resources already at the student's disposal. Therefore, it is crucial to make students aware of their resources.

Available resources must be spelled out directly (topic of interaction). Resources are indirectly an element of the teacher-student relationship. It's not enough to be *told* that I have resources; I must experience it within the relationship with my teacher (observational learning).

Students must experience themselves as *competent* and *able* over and over to achieve reasonable goals because it builds self-efficacy, reduces stress, and allows for successful experiences.[2] While *problem-focused* teaching can be stressful, resource-oriented discussions are generally seen as liberating. They build confidence and hope.

You must learn what the other person's resources are. To get to know these resources, it is helpful to ask for:

- Successes and Achievements
- Skills and Talents
- Social support (family) and positive living situations
- Well-being and Activities (hobbies, interests)
- Motivations and Strengths
- Skills when interacting with other people

More often than not, we tend to focus on problems too much. Our communication is biased towards criticism.[3] To balance it with the opposite (resource-orientation) is very helpful. Here are examples I ask myself before lessons:

- What do I appreciate about the student?
- What are his or her strengths?

- What has she already accomplished?
- What do others like about him?
- What does she like about herself?

Looking deeper at prospective goals, further questions include:

- What does the student expect from me?
- What does she appreciate about me?
- What do I accomplish for him/her?
- What does she expect from me?
- Which aspects of his or her wishes can I fulfill?

Activating resources needs a precise assessment of the other person's individual skills and preferences. Some people like concrete solutions - if you offer a long analysis, the result will not be positive. Others tend to have a rather intellectual and insight-oriented approach to life. They can feel over-burdened when they encounter difficult emotions.

Strengths and competencies may have a negative effect in certain situations and vice versa. It's a good strategy to look deeper into things you perceive as negative - a negative statement can often be reframed into something positive. If you are a musician and have stage fright, it's natural to see this as negative. If you have to perform in any way (give presentations, speak in public), performance anxiety is an obstacle. But there are (among many other layers) some strengths at the bottom of it: the ability to understand *good quality*, the *will* to perform well, and *aspirations* for oneself.

Frequently, I see that students don't acknowledge their achievements and their successes properly. Maybe it's part of a social taboo - speaking about positive aspects of oneself is easily misunderstood as *bragging*. Therefore, it is vital to give students the license to think and talk about themselves positively. They often find that their achievements are not noteworthy, whereas their deficits need to be on full display 24/7. Successes are devalued by thinking negatively about them (deficit orientation). This tendency to focus on the negative is most likely passed on genetically - we have negativity bias by nature.[4]

Because we have a negative bias, we must correct our perception. Resource activation should not be limited solely to the topics at hand but instead, see the student as a whole. Maybe they have resources also somewhere else? Resources in other aspects of life can be very beneficial - they can stabilize the psyche and offer possible solutions. If we have a positive self-image at (let's say) sports, this can positively influence our exam anxiety as well.

Negativity bias: The brain likes to focus on potentially harmful things.

In this light, so-called "small talk" can be very revealing. In a low-key, small-talk interaction, you can learn a lot about the students and what makes them tick. This information then is beneficial in calibrating your educational approaches. Since motivation is key, I often try to find out what students feel very motivated about (TV shows, games, etc.). I try to understand what they appreciate about these shows or games. I was surprised how much you can learn about the other person's needs by understanding what they like.

A key mechanism of learning is observation.[5] As teachers, we function as a model; this role should not be underestimated. The way we act and talk has a great impact. I like to call this *representative appropriation*. People emulate others' behaviors, especially if they hold them in high regard (the leader-follower idea).

It is very important to reflect deeply. Which behaviors, which commentaries, and which self-disclosures serve this modeling function best? Which behavior should we demonstrate to teach it? How should we comment about training how to speak? How much should we open up about ourselves to work on empathy?

Self-disclosures serve as markers for vulnerability - used with care and precision, they offer empathy training for the student. Normally, teachers should be careful with opening up about personal matters. Students are not counselors. The classroom is not group therapy for teachers.

The teacher's individual needs, opinions, values, goals, and experiences are not the prime topic of lessons (this is called *abstinence* in therapy). A different matter altogether is if you make a conscious exception from this rule. This is warranted if you feel that offering specific disclosure may be helpful to the student; it then serves as a modeling function.[6]

Teachers have problems like everyone else.[7] A mastery-model tends to intimidate; a coping-model empowers. A coping-model acknowledges that problems can be solved (as a general rule) *without* the need for perfection. Therefore, it's sometimes very good to tell students that you encountered roadblocks (similar to their experiences) as well.

From a modeling or observational learning viewpoint, your behavior within discussions is very instructional. How do you voice your opinions? How do you argue them? How do you deal with adversarial behavior?

Conditions of observational learning are best fulfilled if you can demonstrate that:

- Problems at hand are not foreign to you (self-disclosure)
- You found a path to solve the problem
- You offer identification (through fostering an emotional relationship)
- You show through your behavior how to solve the problem
- You reinforce students in their attempts to solve problems (respect, praise, sympathy)

In short, it's about demonstrating openness, a positive self-image, and self-reflection.

For example, the fear of speaking in public is normal. It touches on fears of shame and the basic needs of avoiding pain and having control. Teachers have these experiences also. Many problems occur as a heightened form of *normal* human behavior patterns. Use your modeling function. You can talk with the student about your own experiences and how you learned to cope with them. This can be highly motivating, calming, and anxiety-reducing.[8]

There are some vital rules for self-disclosure:

- Make sure that it really benefits the other person.
- Don't use it as an outlet for your own psychological stress.
- Self-disclosure should be applied seldom.
- It should be short.
- Successful coping strategies should be offered.
- These coping strategies should be accessible to the student and within his or her range of competence.

Be careful: If you open up about yourself, boundaries can get blurred. See self-disclosure as a tool, an intervention. It should only be used if you feel comfortable with it.

There are many layers to our personal life. Being careful with self-disclosure, you can be open about the outer layers easily. This allows you to keep the core private. I like telling stories of every-day life with my daughter. By doing so, students experience me as an average person with typical problems, dreams, and anxieties; it helps the coping model.

Apart from self-disclosure, reinforcement is an important activation technique. Reinforcement is a positive reaction, a reward for concrete behavior. We all know this from Pavlov's dog. The basic idea is that behavior will be repeated more often if a positive reward is offered.

For this, teachers can use:

- Attention
- Praise
- Approval as rewards

Unhelpful or destructive behavior should be ignored or be pointed out negatively. The well-aimed use of positive reinforcement (in therapy, it's called *contingency management*) is one of the main tasks for teachers.

When getting to know each other, the teacher's attentiveness, appreciation, and empathy are positive rewards for openness, trust, and hope. In the long run, reinforcement should be focused on *achievements* and changes made. It's important reward not only successes but also those working for change (even when unsuccessful).

Practitioner's Tip:
You can reward by facial expression or gestures (nodding, smiling), short statements ("That's a good idea!"), or through tone of voice (a bit louder, energetic tone). Sentences like "You did very well, respect!" or "Would you had thought a few months ago that you could do this?" or "I don't see it often that someone is as hard-working as you."

I like to think about reinforcement as a kind of cheerleading.[9] When facing long odds, athletes can find courage and determination in being cheered on. Like cheerleaders, teachers can point out strengths, offer options, and appreciate engagement. For example, you can say something like, "You already accomplished so much, more than you thought capable of in the beginning. I know that you will manage the next step also!" or "I have absolute confidence that you will tackle this problem. You have courage and you're determined" or "I believe in you!"

I believe that teachers are generally too reluctant with praise and appreciation. If you don't praise (or too little), you lose an excellent tool for reinforcement. Praise and appreciation for achievements and efforts must be offered directly, emotionally, perceptibly, and distinctly. The positive energy you give can be a great reward.

The reward needs to be attractive. Reinforcement can only work if the reward is seen as enticing. Imagine Pavlov's dog and a bowl of birdfeed — no reinforcement there, right? It's even better if the reward helps the student to reach a goal.

To end reinforcement, it is best to fade out. *Fading* is a method in which you infrequently offer reinforcement (intermittent reinforcement). The student learns to reinforce themself for achievements. In the end, the new behavior does no longer depend on external reinforcement.

Over time, the teacher-student-relationship changes. Invariably, there will be difficult phases - it's a fact of life. *Metacommunication* is a helpful and effective strategy when there are problems. Metacommunication means talking about communication itself. This can help analyze a problem and bring it to focus. A typical question to achieve this is, "What's happening right now? I'm a bit confused and would like to know how you feel."

When you start metacommunication that way, you can further talk about how you experience the situation (in fancy terms, that's called *contingent personal feedback*). It is a technique that confronts the other person with the effect of their behavior. You can report your emotions, thoughts, and impulses. You can say something like, "I felt really disrespected here. To me, respect is very important."

In teaching, you often have to confront learners about problematic parts of themselves (attitudes, thought patterns, emotions, and body movements, un-helpful personal behaviors, etc.). It's an art form in itself to be able to do so without causing harm. I work on it every day. To learn how to confront students helpfully, I strongly recommend taking a class in nonviolent communication or reading Rosenberg's excellent book on the matter.[10]

From a learning perspective, confronting others is necessary. As humans, we tend to avoid uncomfortable thoughts and situations. We need others to point out our failings in a good way; we need benevolent mirrors. I believe that confronting problems doesn't have to feel bad. We can succeed with problem-solving through guided exploration, empathy, and validation, which do not *hurt*.

In psychotherapy training, students are told that acceptance is "the older sister of change." That's certainly true. The thin line to be found here is to offer empathy and validation while at the same time pointing out the need for change. You must show understanding, but at the same time, the *responsibility* for meaningful change stays with the other. In one sentence: Firm on *the matter, sympathetic in tone.* The message should be, "I appreciate you as a person, and my criticism is only aimed at what you do/how you do something."

One advantageous technique to get the sting out of criticism is actually *humor*. Humans have this astonishing ability - they can see very difficult situations with humor and irony. Humor is self-distancing. When I make fun of something, I'm not absorbed by it. It needs an outside look to see the funny side of a situation. By looking at something ironically, you are already on a different level (meta-level).

Humor can signal appreciation to another person. If you're in some sort of confrontation and you can laugh about it together, the conflict is diminished in intensity. Humor can offer a lighter, more distanced, and superior look on things. Humor is a great instrument to change perspective and to put available resources into focus. It allows us to regulate emotions positively, and laughing together about something is fantastic for the mutual relationship.[11] We bond with others by laughing together.

Humor is a form of social maintenance. Especially in groups, laughing together is a powerful bonding exercise - it has interpersonal effects. We tend to like people we had humorous interactions with. A recent study found that humor is associated with closeness and liking.[12] The way people use humor allows us to predict their intelligence.[13] Amazing!

To use humor properly is no simple matter. Humor must be used in a manner boosting self-worth. It should be inclusive, a laughter shared, and be well-calibrated. Ask yourself, "What kind of humor does this situation warrant?" Sometimes, I feel that I fail in this. When I try to be funny, and the other person just looks at me like I just cracked the worst dad-joke ever...

The good news is that humor can be trained. Self-deprecating humor is especially powerful because it subtly inverses hierarchy. By making fun of yourself, you permit others to look at themselves less earnestly. Being overly focused on problems and hyper earnest all the time can actually be harmful to students. On the opposite side, humor can be liberating. Learning needs activation. One of the most beneficial ways to activate is through humor and joined laughter.[14]

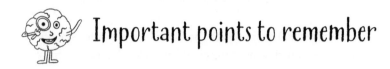# Important points to remember

✓ Leadership doesn't necessarily mean that you have to be in front. You can guide a process by following. The key to success lies in using the resources already at the student's disposal.

✓ See self-disclosure as a tool; it's an intervention. It should only be used if you feel comfortable with it.

✓ Our communication is biased towards criticism. We have negativity bias by nature. If you don't praise (or too little), you lose a great tool for reinforcement.

✓ Acceptance is "the older sister of change." Be firm on the matter, sympathetic in tone.

✓ Learning needs activation. One of the most beneficial ways to activate others is through humor and joined laughter.

Chapter references

1   In Emotion-Focused Therapy, there is a technique for resolving problematic reactions called: systematic evocative unfolding. For further information: Elliott, R., Watson, J., Goldman, R. N., Greenberg, L. S. (2003): *Learning emotion-focused therapy: The process-experiential approach to change.* Washington, DC: American Psychological Association.

2   In psychotherapy, resource-orientation is a well-established research field. See, for example, Willutzki, Ulrike, & Teismann, Tobias, Schulte, Dietmar (2012): "Psychotherapy for Social Anxiety Disorder: Long-Term Effectiveness of Resource-Oriented Cognitive-Behavioral Therapy and Cognitive Therapy in Social Anxiety Disorder." *Journal of Clinical Psychology*, 1-11.

3   See Mantel (2003).

4   See Pinker, Steven (2018): *Enlightenment now. The case for reason, science, humanism, and progress.* New York: Viking.
And Weare, Katherine, Hanh, Thich Nhat (2017): *Happy teachers change the world. A guide for cultivating mindfulness in education.* Berkeley: Parallax Press.

5   See Bandura and his social-cognitive learning theory (1969).

6   For psychotherapy, there is an excellent review here: Henretty J.R. & Levitt H.M. (2010): "The role of therapist self-disclosure in psychotherapy: A qualitative review." *Clinical Psychology Review*, 30, 63–77.

7   See Meichenbaum D. (1971): "Examination of model characteristics in reducing avoidance behavior." *Journal of Personality and Social Psychology*, 14, 298–307.

8   Barrett M. & Berman J. (2001): "Is psychotherapy more effective when therapists disclose information about themselves?" *Journal of Consulting and Clinical Psychology*, 69, 587–603.

9   A concept I found in Lammers, Claas-Hinrich (2017): *Therapeutische Beziehung und Gesprächsführung.* Weinheim: Beltz.

10   Rosenberg, Marshall B. (2005): *Nonviolent Communication: A Language of Life.* Encinitas, CA: PuddleDancer Press.

11   An interesting study is Dezecache, Guillaume & Dunbar, Robin. (2012): "Sharing the Joke: The Size of Natural Laughter Groups." *Evolution and Human Behavior*, 33. 775–779.

12   Treger, Stanislav & Sprecher, Susan & Erber, Ralph (2013): "Laughing and liking: Exploring the interpersonal effects of humor use in initial social interactions." *European Journal of Social Psychology*, 43. 10.1002/ejsp.1962.

13   Howrigan, Daniel (2008): "Humor as a Mental Fitness Indicator." *Evolutionary Psychology*, 6.

14   For more on this matter see Sambanis, Michaela (2013): *Fremdsprachenunterricht und Neurowissenschaften*. Tübingen: Narr Francke Attempto Verlag.

Chapter 23

"The Inner Couch Potato": Motivation, Motivating Communication, and Resistance

Learning needs activation. Motivation is the *activating orientation* towards a positive goal. Motivation is closely linked to hope. I'm motivated to achieve something because I hope to feel better then, to know more, or to be able to do more. It's imperative to be clear about motivations. When we know our motivations, we can commit to a common goal.

Many problems with motivation happen due to a lack of discussion about goals at the outset. When goals are discussed, teachers can set interventions using feedback-loops to realign the techniques with the *intended* goals. Sometimes, goals will change in this process. In the end, success has to be addressed as such.

A lot of frustration for teachers comes when they feel that students simply aren't motivated. It's tough. The problem is that the educational system by itself builds resistance in students. Systems of reward and punishment (good grades, bad grades) can generate great powers of *adversity*. The system forces us to reach certain standards in our education with all the students (that's the fantasy, at least). More often than not, parents put additional pressure on teachers. In my experience, these outside forces are the main reason why the teaching job is so stressful.

Motivation is key because change is hard. Motivation must be high enough, so people are willing to face the strain and the challenge of working on themselves. We should not assume that change is easy for students. Studies have found that teacher and peer support are good for academic motivation.[1]

Sometimes, it comes easy to engage with students.[2] At other times, it is surprisingly hard. Interpersonal skills are vital for success in teaching. In my own teaching, I found that simple things like frequent (brief) eye contact, learning the students' names, and overall taking a real interest in the students go a long way.

As a general rule, students *want to connect* - it is a basic psychological need (attachment). The teachings offered must be relevant to students. In some way, they must relate to students' day-to-day experiences, the problems they face, or concepts they think about. If you can demonstrate that students' contribution is valuable, motivation grows. Inclusive language may also help.

We as teachers need to commit to concrete, practical, and emotional support. It's good to anticipate motivational gaps; failures must be endured. Therefore, motivation is not a static, unmoveable object. Students are not either motivated or unmotivated; instead, it is a dynamic event, a fluctuation.

Motivation is actively *striving* to reach a positive goal. It's not just a wish, but the willingness and the ability to take necessary action. There is a motivation to *seek support* and a *motivation to actively change*. Please do not underestimate the energy needed to do that - change may be most beneficial long-term. Short-term, it is quite costly in most cases. It can involve long hours of practice, insecurity, and the possibility of failure.

If students are ambivalent in their motivation, teachers tend to admonish and administer blame: "The student is not motivated. He/she doesn't want to develop. "It's not for him/her." In my experience, this is not doing justice to the situation. Mostly, shaky motivation points to other problems. Maybe, the student didn't want lessons in the first place! Or maybe there is pressure from the family.

Schulte/Eifert propose a two-fold strategy:[3] a methodology strand and a motivation strand. As long as the other person is motivated, you can use your methods and techniques. When you see that motivation is crumbling, you switch to the motivation strand. You then concentrate on creating positive motivation. When motivation is sufficient again, you switch back to your methods.

Motivation is created by having attractive goals, but attractive goals are not enough. You must also have credible hope that you can reach them. Deci&Ryan (self-determination theory) point out that control is good for motivation.[4] If we feel that we can control the process, we are in charge, and we are motivated.

Motivation is not a given - it's a dynamic process. At one moment, students may be motivated; at another, there is resistance. It can be very frustrating as a teacher when we encounter resistance from our students. We ask ourselves, "We try our best, and we work hard; how can they not appreciate our hard work for them?"

Actually, resistance is a common phenomenon. There are always breaks and glitches in relationships. Teacher-student relationships are no exception to that rule. It's unrealistic to expect they should be different. Look for typical examples of resistance.

For example, when students are:

- Dismissive or overly ironic
- Unpunctual
- Canceling at the last minute
- Interpreting the teacher's statements only negatively
- Being caught in negative thought loops
- Diminishing successes
- Being passive and short in answers

Resistance can have many causes, for example, a feeling of being overwhelmed, too stressed, or insecure. It can also be the case that students feel insufficiently understood and supported by the teacher. Maybe there are factors in the surrounding environment that are harmful (a significant person talking against the teacher), or the teacher uses "correct" techniques (empathy, confrontation) at the wrong moments.

When people feel too dominated and boxed in, they will try to find ways to escape this situation. When students rebel against too much structuring in their lives, this is a form of *reactance*. Reactance is the "motivation to regain freedom after it has been lost or threatened." (Steindl et al., 2015)[5]

This happens when our basic need for autonomy and control is not met. Dominance can have many faces. It can be experienced through unreasonable demands, inappropriate criticism, too much confrontation, or rigidity. Behaviors like that diminish the students' feeling of autonomy.

The essential strategy is to allow students to experience control by following their lead in establishing goals and strategies (as much as possible). I suggest erring on the side of caution. Motivation is easy to break but hard to gain. As a rule of thumb, it's better to follow the student on a path I can't subscribe to 100% than risk losing motivational momentum. (In practice, this can be very difficult. Quick decisions need to be made in class.)

It's very important to keep the basic needs of the other person in mind. Patronizing and pressurizing behavior depletes motivation; controlling and confrontational approaches tend to break the momentum. If I fail to look at the resources at hand, resistance can be the result. Lack of structure and no strategy can also lead to a loss of trust and hope.

Practitioner's Tip:
I've had good experiences with regularly asking, "Are you happy? Is the approach okay for you?" or saying, "I'm just guessing here — please tell me if I'm wrong." In the end, these questions pay off. It's always useful to do relationship maintenance.

Basically, when resistance occurs, you should ask yourself, "What's the benefit for the student at this particular moment?" Students are always motivated towards something - it just might be that they are motivated to do something other than we want. Therefore, resistance is precious information. It can say a lot about the student, their outlook on life, perspective for the future, the relationship to the teacher, etc.

Typical symptoms of resistance include:

- Showing frustration and rejection through posture and facial expressions
- Overall irritated and angry

There are two main aspects to this kind of behavior. It is either characterized by withdrawal (passive, silent, overly aligned to others) or attack (anger, accusations, demands).[6]
    Learning is often highly charged with emotions. It frequently happens during vulnerable, critical periods of personal development. Imagine, for example, you are unemployed and are training for a new career. Of course, you're not learning out of pure joy. Many different emotions are intertwined.[7]

Besides positive emotions, students may also encounter (on the more difficult end of the scale):

- Anxiety
- Loneliness
- Helplessness
- Guilt

They can think that "people don't like me, people don't take me seriously, no one understands me, no one listens to me, people just want me to function, I'm not loveable, or I'm stupid and ugly."

To better understand resistance, I recommend going through the three components of *coherence* (Bordin 1979). If we align in *goals, tasks* and through an *affective* relationship, we are on a good path. Ask yourself, "What are our goals right now? The tasks? How is the relationship?"

Rather than addressing resistance openly, I suggest backtracking in the process. Try analyzing again what the motives of the other person are. More often than not, the quality of the relationship *doesn't allow* working on the resistance directly. Calling the other person out can already be too much confrontation.

If there is a chance to address resistance covertly, I recommend doing so. Reassess your techniques and the overall strategy. Look at the relationship. Does the other person react positively to empathy and validation? Or does he/she need a more active approach? Do you need to press for change? Or rather, should you help to manage difficult emotions?

Many people have mixed feelings about change. In psychology, this is called "motivational ambivalence." If motivation problems are at the center of resistance, motivating communication is a useful and well-established tool.[8] Especially in the beginning, when still in the process of establishing a good relationship, ambivalence is normal. If teachers press too much for change or are too aggressive, less motivation will result.

Often, we act too fast. This happens if we do not look closely at the other person's motivational state. The danger is great if we try to do too many things, give too much input, or push too much for change without properly preparing the ground. Often, it's better to make a change by strengthening the relationship basis.

A helpful strategy is to try to make the student an *advocate for change*. It's best to help them develop motivation from their own inner resources. Motivating communication is focused on exploring the other person's motivations and resources within a framework of partnership. It's necessary to understand what makes the other person tick. Ask yourself, "What are his or her motivations (intrinsic)? What is the personality like? What are his/her goals and the underlying values? What is their meaning?"

Intrinsic (solely coming out of him or herself) motivation is center stage. The opposite, extrinsic motivation (especially pressure from the outside, family, friends, partners, etc.) remains in the background. More often than not, extrinsic motivation backfires. Pressure and accusations work well but lead to feelings of anxiety, guilt, and shame. These emotions lessen motivation and resistance increases. It's not a suitable path. Sentences like, "You must do XYZ. If you go on like this, you will fail. You promised to change," are not helpful (even if they may be correct). It's better to choose:

- Partnership over confrontation, a cooperative relationship.
- Evocation over advice. The other person has the motivation and the resources needed to change. These resources need to be called into existence (evoked).
- Autonomy over authority. The other person has the right to be self-determined. He or she can decide what's going to happen.

Motivational communication aims to avoid *dissonance*. Dissonance mostly arises from:

- Having differing goals
- Being too confrontational
- Being (excessively) demanding
- Not being respectful
- Deciding things alone
- Not being understanding enough

Communication based on partnership wants to achieve a high degree of consonance. At the end of the day, we must work together and not against each other. Consonance means that the other person has the chance to develop insight, understanding, and acceptance of realities by him or herself.

If too much pressure is applied, it's likely the other person will clam up and protect his or her self-worth by resisting change. Imagine that you're not facing each other but sitting side-by-side. You try to see problems and challenges the way the other person does.

Motivational communication has two phases. First, we need to boost general change motivation. Then we can select concrete goals, paths, and plans for change. Four principles are vital:[9]

- **Empathy:**
  Trying to see things from the other's perspective and understanding resistance and ambivalence.
- **Addressing *discrepancies*:**
  Leading the other to the awareness that there is a gap between what's present and their aspirations.
- **Going with *resistance*:**

Resistance is not only an obstacle; it's also very useful information

- **Strengthen *self-efficacy*:**
  If the other person experiences strengths, competencies, and resources often enough, this will change the self-image.

The responsibility for change always lies with the other person. He or she is self-determined after all. As teachers, we often work under outside restrictions (syllabus), which greatly diminishes our wriggle room. But at the end of the day, it's the students' responsibility to learn.

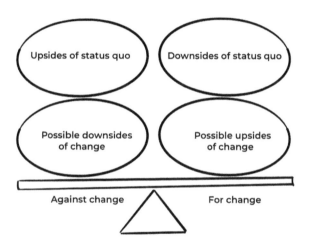

Decision matrix "upsides and downsides of change".

Resistance, resisting change, and resisting insights have *benefits* for the individual. If I resist change, I can spare a lot of effort and energy. (Of course, that's not a good strategy in the long run.) Change tends to occur when the comparative cost of not changing becomes too great (pain threshold).

If you understand that staying in the current state has benefits (from the person's perspective), you can better help the student. As I said, change is difficult and needs a lot of courage. Often, resistance is not lacking will-power, but a lack of *positive experiences with change* in the past. Self-efficacy will make that better. If I trust my own ability to drive meaningful change forward, it's easier to do so.

That's the core of teaching (in my opinion) - instigate change, give support through expert knowledge, and boost self-efficacy. If we can help others explore their talents, we also help them push their limits. I believe that we, as a society, too often settle for too little. Mediocrity has its merits. By staying within confined limits, we don't expose ourselves.

Risking exposure needs courage and strength. This is the gold standard of any educational endeavor - to help others reach further than they thought possible, to stretch their imaginations of what they could do, and, in the end, to help them *empower themselves.*

Important points to remember

✓ Motivation is not a given. It's a dynamic process. Students are always motivated (maybe to do something else than we want).

✓ Interpersonal skills are vital for success. We as teachers need to commit to concrete, practical, and emotional support.

✓ Resistance is a common phenomenon.

✓ Learning frequently happens during vulnerable, critical periods of personal development.

✓ Motivating communication is focused on exploring the other person's motivations and resources within a framework of partnership. Communication based on partnership aims at a high degree of consonance.

Chapter references

1   See Kiefer, Sarah M., Alley, Kathleen M., Ellerbrock, Cheryl R. (2015): "Teacher and Peer Support for Young Adolescents' Motivation, Engagement, and School Belonging" *RMLE Online*, 38 (8).

2   Especially structured voluntary activities (sports, arts) offer a great chance to develop intrinsic motivation and initiative. See Larson, Reed W. (2000): "Toward a Psychology of Positive Youth Development." *American Psychologist*, 55 (1), 170-183.

3   Schulte D. & Eifert G.H. (2002): "What to do when manuals fail? The dual model of psychotherapy." *Clinical Psychology: Science and Practice*, 9, 312–328.

4   See Deci, Edward L., Ryan, Richard M. (2000): "Self-Determination Theory and the Facilitation of Intrinsic Motivation, Social Development, and Well-being." *American Psychologist*, 55 (1), 68-78.

5   See Steindl, Christina, Jonas, Eva, Sittenthaler, Sandra, Traut-Mausch, Eva, Greenberg, Jeff (2015): "Understanding Psychological Reactance. New Developments and Findings." *Zeitschrift für Psychologie*, 223(4), 205-214.

6   Safran J.D. & Muran J.C. (2006): "Has the concept of therapeutic alliance outlived its usefulness?" *Psychotherapy: Theory, Research, Practice, Training*, 43, 2860–291.

7   The same is true during puberty. Later, we tend to romanticize high school (at least, many people do). In reality, it's a stressful and demanding time for all of us

8   See Hall, Katie, Gibbie, Tania, Lubman, Dan I. (2012): "Motivational interviewing techniques. Facilitating behavior change in the general practice setting." *Australian Family Physician*, 41 (9).

9   See Arkowitz H., Westra H.A., Miller W.R., Rollnick S. (2010): *Motivierende Gesprächsführung bei der Behandlung psychischer Störungen*. Weinheim: Beltz.

Epilogue

This is the end of my book.

Studies and research are one thing; I quoted many.

But real life tends to be a teacher of its own. I would like this epilogue to be my personal summary of the points I personally find most important and the things I learned over the years.

I put my favorite quote from David Deutsch at the beginning: *"Everything that is not forbidden by laws of nature is achievable, given the right knowledge."* I like this quote a lot. It took me a long time to really understand its significance.

This quote shows two things: First, that we can achieve a lot. Second, that knowledge is the key to do so. For me, as a teacher, that's good news. I'm in the *bringing-knowledge-to-people business*, after all!

On a deeper level, knowledge is not just "stuff we learned from others" or lessons we've gleaned from people in authority or from teachers we revere. It is also our duty to test. We should accept statements only as true as long as they are not disproven.

For progress, a culture of critical reflection and testing is crucial - try something out, learn from it, and repeat the process. If you go on as you have always gone, the result will be *identical*. If what you're trying doesn't work, you must find a different approach. This may sound *simple*, but it is by no means easy.

There's *honesty* in it. It means to accept the consequences of what we do. It entails not making *excuses* or blaming others.

There is *integrity* in it - a culture of critical thinking and testing allows for *failure*.

The only real failure is not to try. If you understand this, then failures turn into learning experiences. We should expect mistakes and welcome them. Mistakes are a sign that we learn - that we get better. This may sound like a cheap sales pitch in a motivational video, but, nevertheless, it's true. I learned most from the setbacks I had to live through.

There is a lot of power in how you look at these situations. If you regard mistakes as proof that you are a failure, you will have no energy for change. If you try to avoid setbacks, you will flatten your learning curve, and you will learn much less. As a teacher, you are your own student, first and foremost. Teach yourself like you (would like to) teach your students.

The basic idea is to start with something small, obtain wins, and build more demanding tasks on this success. This way, the process will be enjoyable. Change can actually be fun when managed in this manner. When working with students, set small goals within reach (quite) easily and highlight successes. Work on weaker traits, and find arenas to show the students' skills. I spend a considerable amount of time trying to find suitable places for students to experience their progress. It's vital for motivation, self-efficacy, and self-worth.

The whole last part of this book is about communication. When we speak with others, we indirectly signal who we are. We like to connect to other people we see as warm and competent. We have underlying traits (honesty, knowledge, wisdom), making other people want to connect with us. We should think about others and ourselves in this manner. Do I see myself as warm and competent? Do I see others like that? How do they behave?

The way I see it, the society we live in has a lot of in-built violence; warmth and competence are good traits to show in an environment like this. Violence can have many shapes - it can be physical or emotional. Gandhi believed that the scars left by emotional violence run even deeper than the harm inflicted by physical violence.[1] We should not underestimate emotional cruelty. It can bend the trajectory of a whole personality out of shape.

In confronting the effects of violence, healing is necessary. The good news is that healing is not only *necessary*; it is also *possible*.

We tend to accept a lot of violent behavior around us simply because it has been like this for a long time. If our world seems ruthless to you, it was made so by our attitudes. I believe that we can change our attitudes, and by doing so, we bring (a little) change to society. This whole book is written from the viewpoint of support and understanding.

I stress understanding and motivation a lot.

Motivation is understanding what the other person aspires to and why. In looking for others' motivations, there is already a high degree of respect. Motivation is the opposite of manipulation. Where motivation tries to lift others up and to help them reach their goals, manipulation makes others conform to the goals set out for them. I believe manipulation to be demeaning; it harms the human spirit.

And manipulation is everywhere around us.

The only way I know to start changing in this regard is by looking at how we speak with others. I would like to propose the following **maxims**, which have been a guiding star in my own teaching for years:

- Make sure that students have as many positive experiences in class as possible.
- Offer well-aimed praise and appreciation.
- Use small steps, leading to many small successes.
- Try to understand the other's motivation.
- Work on your difficult emotions rather than showing them.
- Try to end lessons always on a positive-affective note and allow for bonding.
- During lessons, ask yourself what the other person may experience at this moment.
- Not only reflect on *what* you say but especially on *how* you say it.
- Always keep in mind the basic psychological needs of the other person.

That's it.

People like to say, "You should never inspect the kitchen at your favorite restaurant. You might not want to eat there afterward!" Having written this book, I feel exactly the same. I've shown you my kitchen, and I very much hope that (after touring it) you still like to eat here.

Thank you very much.

Chapter references

1   See Rosenberg, Marshall B. (2005): *Nonviolent Communication: A Language of Life*. Encinitas, CA: PuddleDancer Press.

References

Abramowitz, Jonathan S.; Deacon, Brett J.; Whiteside, Stephen P. H. (2011-03-14). *Exposure Therapy for Anxiety: Principles and Practice.* Guilford Press. ISBN 9781609180171.

Alison, Emily, Alison, Laurence J. (2020): Rapport: *The Four Ways to Read People.* London: Vermilion.

Allen, Jon G./ Fonagy, Peter (Hrsg.) (2006): Handbook of mentalization-based treatment. Chichester: John Wiley & Sons Ltd.

Anderson T., Ogles B.M., Patterson C.L., Lambert M.J., Vermeersch D.A. (2009): "Therapist effects: Facilitative interpersonal skills as a predictor of therapist success." *Journal of Clinical Psychology*, 65, 755–768.

Arkowitz H., Westra H.A., Miller W.R., Rollnick S. (2010): Motivierende Gesprächsführung bei der Behandlung psychischer Störungen. Weinheim: Beltz.

Bandura, Albert (1969): *Principles of behavior modification.* New York: Holt, Rinehart and Winston.

Bandura, Albert (1982). "Self-efficacy mechanism in human agency." *American Psychologist.* 37 (2): 122–147.

Barrett M. & Berman J. (2001): "Is psychotherapy more effective when therapists disclose information about themselves?" *Journal of Consulting and Clinical Psychology*, 69, 587–603.

Bates, A. W. (Tony) (2019): *Teaching in a Digital Age. Guidelines for designing teaching and learning.* Vancouver: BCcampus.

Bauer, Joachin (2010): *Das Gedächtnis des Körpers. Wie Beziehungen und Lebensstile unsere gene steuern*. Frankfurt/Main: Eichborn.

Bäuml, Karl-Heinz/Pastötter, Bernhard/ Hanslmayr, Simon (2010): "Binding and inhibition in episodic memory-Cognitive, emotional, and neural processes." *Neuroscience & Biobehavioral Reviews*, 34, 7, 1047-1054.

Bischkopf J. (2013): *Emotionsfokussierte Therapie*. Göttingen: Hogrefe.

Bodenhamer, Bob G., Hall, Michael L. (1999): *The User's Manual for The Brain*. Carmarthen: Crown House Publishing.

Böhnlein, Joscha; Altegoer, Luisa; Muck, Nina Kristin; Roesmann, Kati; Redlich, Ronny; Dannlowski, Udo; Leehr, Elisabeth J. (2020): "Factors influencing the success of exposure therapy for specific phobia: A systematic review." *Neuroscience & Biobehavioral Reviews*, 108: 796–820.

Bordin E. S. (1979): "The generalizability of the psychoanalytic concept of the working alliance." *Psychotherapy: Theory, Research & Practice*, 16, 252–260.

Bratman, Michael E. (2004): *Faces of Intention. Selected Essays on Intention and Agency*. Cambridge: Cambridge University Press.

Butzkamm, Wolfgang (2012): *Lust zum Lehren, Lust zum Lernen: Eine neue Methodik für den Fremdsprachenunterricht*. Tübingen: Francke.

Castonguay L.G., Constantino M.J. & Clarke H., Rees A. & Hardy Ggrosse Holtforth M. (2006): "The working alliance: Where are we and where should we go?" *Psychotherapy*, 43, 271–279.

Castro, Dotan R., Kluger, Avraham N., Itzchakov, Guy (2016): "Does avaoidance-attachment style attenuate the benefits of being listened to?" *European Journal of Social Psychology*, 46, 6.

Cataudella, Stefania & Lampis, Jessica & Busonera, Alessandra & L., Marino & Zavattini, Giulio Cesare. (2016): "From parental-fetal attachment to a parent-infant relationship: A systematic review about prenatal protective and risk factors." *Life Span and Disability*. XIX. 185-219.

Chubbuck, Ivana (2004): *The Power of the Actor*. New York: Gotham books.

Coussons-Read, Mary (2013): "Effects of prenatal stress on pregnancy and human development: Mechanisms and pathways." *Obstetric Medicine: The Medicine of Pregnancy*, 6. 52-57. 10.1177/1753495X12473751.

Cowley, Sue (2009): *Teaching Skills for Dummies*. Chichester: John Wiley & Sons, Ltd.

Curran, T., & Hill, A. (2019): "Perfectionism Is Increasing Over Time: A Meta-Analysis of Birth Cohort Differences From 1989 to 2016."*Psychological Bulletin*, 145, 410–429.

Curtis R., Field C., Knaan-Kostmann L., Mannis K. (2014): "What 75 psychoanalysts found helpful and hurtful in their own analysis." *Psychoanalytic Psychology*, 21, 183–202.

Damasio, A.R.; Tranel, D.; Damasio, H.C. (1991). "Ch. 11: Somatic markers and the guidance of behaviour: theory and preliminary testing." Levin, Harvey S.; Eisenberg, Howard M.; Benton, Arthur Lester (eds.): *Frontal Lobe Function and Dysfunction*. Oxford: Oxford University Press. pp. 217–229.

Damasio, Antonio R. (2008): *Descartes' Error: Emotion, Reason and the Human Brain*. New York: Random House.

Dassler, Henning (1999): "Emotion und pädagogische Professionalität: Die Bedeutung des Umgangs mit Gefühlen für sozialpädagogische Berufe." URL:http://digisrv-1.biblio.etc. tu-bs.de:8080/docportal/servlets/MCRFileNodeServlet/ DocPortal_derivate_00001104/ Document.pdf [Stand 25.05.2020].

Deci, Edward L., Ryan, Richard M. (2000): "Self-Determination Theory and the Facilitation of Intrinsic Motivation, Social Development, and Well-being." *American Psychologist*, 55 (1), 68-78.

Deutsch, David (2011): *The Beginning of Infinity: Explanations That Transform the World*. London: Penguin.

Doty, James R. (2016): *Into the Magic Shop: A Neurosurgeon's Quest to Discover the Mysteries of the Brain and the Secrets of the Heart*. New York: Avery.

Einsle F. & Hummel K.V. (2015): *Kognitive Umstrukturierung*. Weinheim: Beltz.

Elliott, R., Watson, J., Goldman, R. N., Greenberg, L. S. (2003): *Learning emotion-focused therapy: The process-experiential approach to change*. Washington, DC: American Psychological Association.

Elliot R., Bohart A.C., Watson J.C. & Greenberg L.S. (2011): "Empathy" *Psychotherapy: Theory, Research, Practice, Training*, 48, 43–49.

Epstein, Seymour (2003): Cognitive-Experiential Self-Theory of Personality. *Handbook of psychology: Personality and social psychology*, Vol. 5. Million, Theodore (Ed.); Lerner, Melvin J. (Ed.); Hoboken, NJ, US: John Wiley & Sons Inc.

Feynman, Richard P. (1985): *"Surely You're Joking, Mr. Feynman!" Adventures of a Curious Character*. New York: W. W. Norton Company.

Finkel, E., Hui, C.M., Carswell, K.L., & Larson, G.M. (2014): "The Suffocation of Marriage: Climbing Mount Maslow Without Enough Oxygen." *Psychological Inquiry*, 25, 1 - 41.

Fisk, Susa T., Cuddy, Amy J.C., Glick, Peter (2007): "Universal dimensions of social cognition: warmth and competence." *TRENDS in Cognitive Sciences*, 11 (2).

Flückiger C., DelRe A.C., Wampol D.E., Znoj H.,Caspar F. & Jörg U. (2012): "Valuing clients' perspective and the effects on the therapeutic alliance: A randomized controlled study of an adjunctive instruction." *Journal of Counseling Psychotherapy*, 59, 18–26.

Fonagy, Peter, Target, Mary (2002): "Neubewertung der Entwicklung der Affektregulation vor dem Hintergrund von Winnicotts Konzept des »falschen Selbst«." *Psyche-Z Psychoanal*, 56, 839–862.

Frank, Robert H. (2016): *Success and luck. Good fortune and the myth of meritocracy*. Princeton: Princeton University Press.

Gassmann D. & Grawe K. (2006): "General change mechanisms: The relation between problem activation and ressource activation in successful and unsuccessful therapeutic interactions." *Clinical Psychology and Psychotherapy*, 13, 1–11.

Gazzaley, A.,& Rosen, L.D. (2016): *The Distracted Mind: Why Technology Hijacks Our Brain and How to Enhance Our Focus Amidst the Noise*. Cambridge, Massachusetts: MIT Press.

Gilbert, Paul (2010): "An Introduction to Compassion Focused therapy in Cognitive Behavior Therapy." *International Journal of Cognitive Therapy*, 3 (2), 97-112.

Grawe K. & Grawe-Gerber M. (1999): "Ressourcenaktivierung" *Psychotherapeut*, 44, 63–73.

Grawe, Klaus (2004): *Neuropsychotherapie*. Göttingen: Hogrefe-Verlag.

Grossmann, Karin; Grossmann, Klaus E. (2012): *Bindungen. Das Gefüge psychischer Sicherheit*. 5. Aufl. Stuttgart: Klett-Cotta.

Haarhoff B. (2006): "The importance of identifying and understanding therapist schema in cognitive therapy training and supervision." *New Zealand Journal of Psychology*, 35,126–131.

Hall, Katie, Gibbie, Tania, Lubman, Dan I. (2012): "Motivational interviewing techniques. Facilitating behavior change in the general practice setting." *Australian Family Physician*, 41 (9).

Henretty J.R. & Levitt H.M. (2010): "The role of therapist self-disclosure in psychotherapy: A qualitative review." *Clinical Psychology Review*, 30, 63–77.

Herculano-Houzel, Suzana (2009): "The Human Brain in Numbers: A Linearly Scaled-up Primate Brain." *Frontiers in Human Neuroscience*, 3, 31.

Hezel, Dianne M.; Simpson, H. Blair (2019): "Exposure and response prevention for obsessive-compulsive disorder: A review and new directions." *Indian Journal of Psychiatry*, 61 (Suppl 1): S85–S92.

Hölzel BK, Carmody J, Evans KC, et al. (2010): "Stress reduction correlates with structural changes in the amygdala." *Soc Cogn Affect Neurosci*.;5(1):11-17.

Hou, Youbo & Xiong, Dan & Jiang, Tonglin & Song, Lili & Wang, Qi. (2019): "Social media addiction: Its impact, mediation, and intervention." *Cyberpsychology: Journal of Psychosocial Research on Cyberspace*. 13. 10.5817/CP2019-1-4.

Howrigan, Daniel (2008): "Humor as a Mental Fitness Indicator." *Evolutionary Psychology*, 6. 10.1177/147470490800600411.

Hüther, Gerald (2011): *Was wir sind und was wir sein könnten. Ein neurobiologischer Mutmacher*. 2. Auflage. Frankfurt/Main: S. Fischer Verlag.

Hwang, Yoon-Suk, Medvedev, Oleg N., Krägeloh, Chris, Hand, Kirstine, Noh, 1&Jae-Eun, Singh, Nirbhay N. (2019): "The Role of Dispositional Mindfulness and Self-compassionin Educator Stress." *Mindfulness*, 10:1692–1702

Jood, K., Redfors, P., Rosengren, A., Blomstrand, C., & Jern, C. (2009). Self-perceived psychological stress and ischemic stroke: a case-control study. *BMC medicine*, 7, 53.

Jung, C.G. (1996): *The Archetypes and the Collective Unconscious*. London. Routledge.

Kabat-Zinn J. (2003): "Mindfulness-based interventions in context: past, present, and future." *Clin. Psychol.-Sci. Practice* 144–156.

Kabat-Zinn, Jon (2005): *Wherever You Go, There You Are*. New York: Hachette Books.

Kafka, Franz (1995): *The Complete Stories*. New York: Schocken; Reprint Edition

Kandel, Eric (2007): *In Search of Memory: The Emergence of a New Science of Mind*. New York: Norton & Company.

Kandel, Eric (2016): *Reductionism in Art and Brain Science. Bridging the Two Cultures*. New York: Columbia University Press.

Kaufman, Scott Barry (2020): Transcend. The New Science of Self-Actualization. New York, NY: TarcherPerigee.

Kemp, Simon, Burt, Christopher D. B., Furneaux, Laura (2008): "A test of the peak-end rule with extended autobiographical events." *Memory & Cognition*, 36 (1) 132-138.

Kiefer, Sarah M., Alley, Kathleen M., Ellerbrock, Cheryl R. (2015): "Teacher and Peer Support for Young Adolescents' Motivation, Engagement, and School Belonging." *RMLE Online*, 38 (8).

Killingsworth, Matthew A., Gilbert, Daniel T. (2010): "A Wandering Mind Is an Unhappy Mind." Science, Vol. 330, Issue 6006, pp. 932.

Klawe, Willy(2008): "Individualpädagogische Maßnahmen als tragfähiges Beziehungsangebot. Ergebnisse einer empirischen Studie." Unsere Jugend (5):208–217. URL:http://www.shnetz.de/klawe/archiv/Individualpaedagogik/Individualpaedagogik_als_Beziehung.pdf [downloaded 24.11.2019]

Kloss, Sherry (2000): *Jascha Heifetz. Through my eyes.* Muncie, Indiana: Kloss Classics/ Ball State University.

Kühn, S., Gleich, T., Lorenz, R. C., Lindenberger, U., & Gallinat, J. (2014): "Playing Super Mario induces structural brain plasticity: Gray matter changes resulting from training with a commercial video game." *Molecular Psychiatry*, 19, 265-271.

Lally, P., Jaarsveld, C.V., Potts, H., & Wardle, J. (2010): "How are habits formed: Modelling habit formation in the real world." *European Journal of Social Psychology*, 40, 998-1009.

Lally, P., & Gardner, B. (2013): "Promoting habit formation." *Health Psychology Review*, 7, 137 - 158.

Lammers, Claas-Hinrich (2017): *Therapeutische Beziehung und Gesprächsführung.* Weinheim: Beltz.

Laneri, D., Schuster, V., Dietsche, B., Jansen, A., Ott, U., & Sommer, J. (2016): "Effects of Long-Term Mindfulness Meditation on Brain's White Matter Microstructure and its Aging." *Frontiers in aging neuroscience*, 7, 254.

Larson, Reed W. (2000): "Toward a Psychology of Positive Youth Development." *American Psychologist*, 55 (1), 170-183.

Lazarus, Richard S. (1991). "Progress on a cognitive-motivational-relational theory of Emotion." *American Psychologist*, 46(8), 819-834.

Lazarus, Richard S (2000): "Toward Better Research on Stress and Coping." *American Psychologist*, Vol. 55. No. 6, 665 673.

LeDoux, Joseph (2016): *Anxious: Using the Brain to Understand and Treat Fear and Anxiety.* New York, NY: Penguin Random House.

Lewin, Kurt (1935): *A Dynamic Theory of Personality.* New York: McGraw-Hill.

Linden, David J. (2011): *Pleasure: how our brains make junk food, exercise, marijuana, generosity, and gambling feel so good.* Richmond: Oneworld.

Lohmann, B. (2017): *Selbstunterstützung für Psychotherapeuten.* Göttingen: Hogrefe.

Malancharuvil, JM (2004): "Projection, introjection, and projective identification: a reformulation." *American Journal of Psychoanalysis*, 64 (4): 375–82.

Mantel, Gerhard (2003): *Mut zum Lampenfieber. Mentale Strategien für Musiker zur Bewältigung von Auftritts- und Prüfungsangst*. Mainz: Serie Musik Atlantis, Schott.

Martin D.J., Garske J.P. & Davis M.K. (2000): "Relation of the therapeutic alliance with outcome and other variables: A meta-analytic review." *Journal of Consulting and Clinical Psychology*, 68, 438–450.

Maslow, Abraham (1954). *Motivation and personality*. New York, NY: Harper.

Maslow, Abraham H. (1996). "Critique of self-actualization theory." E. Hoffman (ed.). *Future visions: The unpublished papers of Abraham Maslow*. Thousand Oaks, CA: Sage.

McCarthy, Gabby (2018): *Introduction to Metaphysics*. Waltham Abbey: ED-Tech Press.

McCorry, LK (2007): "Physiology of the autonomic nervous system." *American Journal of Pharmaceutical Education*, 71 (4): 78.

Meichenbaum D. (1971): "Examination of model characteristics in reducing avoidance behavior." *Journal of Personality and Social Psychology*, 14, 298–307.

Merten J. (2001): *Beziehungsregulation in der Psychotherapie. Maladaptive Beziehungsmuster und der therapeutische Prozess*. Stuttgart: Kohlhammer.

Messer S.B. & Wampold B.E. (2002): "Let's face facts: Common factors are more potent than specific therapy ingredients," *American Psychological Association*, 9, 21–25.

Munuera, J., Rigotti, M. & Salzman, C.D. (2018): "Shared neural coding for social hierarchy and reward value in primate amygdala," *Nature Neuroscience* 21, 415–423.

Naumann, laura P., Vazire,Simine, Rentfrow, Peter J., Gosling, Samuel D. (2009): "Personality Judgments Based on Physical Appearance." *Pers Soc Psychol Bull*, 35; 1661.

Norcross, J. C., Lambert, M. J. (2011): Evidence-based therapy relationships. Norcross, J. C. (Ed.): *Psychotherapy relationships that work* (2nd ed.). New York: Oxford University Press.

Ocha E. & Muran J.C. (2008): "A relational take on termination in cognitive-behavioral therapy." W.T. O'Donohue & M.A. Cucciare (Eds.): *Terminating Psychotherapy*. New York: Routledge.

Oevermann, Ulrich.(2009): "Theoretische Skizze einer revidierten Theorie professionalisierten Handelns." *Pädagogische Professionalität. Untersuchungen zum Typus pädagogischen Handelns*. Edited by Arno Combe and Werner Helsper. Frankfurt am Main: Suhrkamp (Suhrkamp-Taschenbuch Wissenschaft, 1230).

Panksepp, Jaak (2012): *The Archaeology of Mind: Neuroevolutionary Origins of Human Emotion*. New York: W.W. Norton & Company.

Persson, Roland S. (1995): "Psychosocial stressors among student musicians: A naturalistic study of the teacher-student relationship." IJAM 4 (2), 7-13.

Persson, Roland S. (1996a): "Studying with a Musical Maestro: A Case Study of Commonsense Teaching in Artistic Training." *Creativity Research Journal*, 9 (1), 33-46.

Persson, Roland S. (1996b): "Brilliant Performers as teachers: a case study of commonsense teaching in a conservatoire setting." *Journal of Music Education*, 28 (1), 25-36.

Pinker, Steven (2018): *Enlightenment now. The case for reason, science, humanism, and progress*. New York: Viking.

Portmann, Adolf (1956): *Zoologie und das neue Bild des Menschen. Biologische Fragmente zu einer Lehre vom Menschen*. Frankfurt: Rowohlt.

Price, Michael E., VanVugt, Mark (2014): "The evolution of leader–follower reciprocity: the theory of service-for-prestige." *Frontiers in Human Neuroscience*, 8 363.

Rheinberg, Falco (2018): *Motivation*. Stuttgart: Kohlhammer Verlag.

Rice L.N. & Saperia E. (1984): "Task analysis of the resolution of problematic reaction." L.N. Rice & L.S. Greenberg (Eds.): *Patterns of change: Intensive analysis of psychotherapy process* (pp. 29–66). New York: Guilford.

Rieser, Fabian (2015): *Experts as Effective Teachers. Understanding the Relevance of Cognition, Emotion, and Relation in Education*. Lanham: Rowman & Littlefield.

Rodenburg, Patsy (2012): "How to develop great performing presence." *The Strad* 122 (5), 52-57.

Rosenberg, Marshall B. (2005): Nonviolent Communication: *A Language of Life*. Encinitas, CA: PuddleDancer Press.

Ruch, Floyd L./Zimbardo, Philip G.(1974): *Lehrbuch der Psychologie. Eine Einführung für Studenten der Psychologie, Medizin und Pädagogik*. Berlin: Springer.

Sachse R. (2015). *Therapeutische Beziehungsgestaltung*. Göttingen: Hogrefe.

Safran J.D. & Muran J.C. (2006): "Has the concept of therapeutic alliance outlived its usefulness?" *Psychotherapy: Theory, Research,Practice, Training*, 43, 2860–291.

Sambanis, Michaela (2013): *Fremdsprachenunterricht und Neurowissenschaften*. Tübingen: Narr Francke Attempto Verlag.

Schaal, Karine et al. (2011): "Psychological Balance in High Level Athletes: Gender-Based Differences and Sport-Specific Patterns." *PLoS One* 4;6(5):e19007.

Schirp, H. (2009): Wie ,lernt' unser Gehirn Werte und Orientierungen? Herrmann, U. (Hrsg.): *Neurodidaktik. Grundlagen und Vorschläge für gehirngerechtes Lehren und Lernen*. Weinheim und Basel: Beltz

Schaef; Anne Wilson (2004): *Meditations for Women Who Do Too Much*. San Francisco: HarperOne.

Scherer, Klaus R. (2005): "What are emotions? And how can they be measured?" *Social Science Information* 44(4), 695–729.

Schnarch, David (2011): *Intimacy and Desire*. New York: Beaufort books.

Schulte D. (1996): *Therapieplanung*. Göttingen: Hogrefe.

Schulte D. & Eifert G.H. (2002): "What to do when manuals fail? The dual model of psychotherapy." *Clinical Psychology: Science and Practice*, 9, 312–328.

Schunk, Dave H., Pintrich, Paul R., Meece, Judith L. (2013): *Motivation in education: Theory, research and applications*. Upper Saddle River, N.J.: Pearson education International.

Searle, John R. (2009): Kollektive Absichten und Handlungen. Schmid, Hans Bernhard/ Schweikard, David P. (Hrsg.) (2009): *Kollektive Intentionalität. Eine Debatte über die Grundlage des Sozialen*. Frankfurt/ Main: Suhrkamp Verlag, 99-118.

Segal, Robert A. (1999): *Theorizing about myth*. Amherst: University of Massachusetts Press.

Senay, Ibrahim/Albarracín, Dolores/Noguchi Kenji: "Motivating Goal-Directed Behavior Through Introspective Self-Talk: The Role of the Interrogative Form of Simple Future Tense." *Psychological Science*, 21, 4, 499-504.

Smith, Craig A., & Kirby, Leslie D. (2009): "Putting appraisal in context: Toward a relational model of appraisal and emotion." *Cognition and Emotion*, 23 (7), 1352–1372.

Sockolov, Matthew (2018): *Practicing Mindfulness: 75 Essential Meditations to Reduce Stress, Improve Mental Health, and Find Peace in the Everyday*. Emeryville: Althea Press.

Sprick, Ulrich (2017): "Psychotherapy via the Internet as a Novel Tool for Clinical Use." *Systemics, Cybernetics and Informatics*, 15 (6).

Steindl, Christina, Jonas, Eva, Sittenthaler, Sandra, Traut-Mausch, Eva, Greenberg, Jeff (2015): "Understanding Psychological Reactance. New Developments and Findings." *Zeitschrift für Psychologie*, 223(4), 205-214.

Stumm, Gerhard, Pritz, Alfred (2009): *Wörterbuch der Psychotherapie*. Vienna, New York: Springer.

Sucala M., Schnur J.B., Constantino M.J., Miller S.J., Brackman E.H. & Montgomery G.H. (2012): "The therapeutic relationship in e-therapy for mental health: A systematic review." *Journal of Medical Internet Research*, 14, e110.

Svenson, Ola, Maule, A. John (1993): *Time Pressure and Stress in Human Judgment and Decision Making*. New York: Springer US.

Swift J.K. & Derthick A.O. (2013): "Increasing hope by addressing clients' outcome expectancies." *Psychotherapy*, 50, 284–287.

Treger, Stanislav & Sprecher, Susan & Erber, Ralph (2013): "Laughing and liking: Exploring the interpersonal effects of humor use in initial social interactions." *European Journal of Social Psychology*, 43. 10.1002/ejsp.1962.

Tuckman, Bruce W. (1965): "Developmental Sequence in Small Groups." *Psychological Bulletin*, 63 (6), 384-399.

Tuomela, Raimo/ Miller, Kaarlo (2009): Wir-Absichten. Schmid, Hans Bernhard/ Schweikard, David P. (Hrsg.) (2009): *Kollektive Intentionalität. Eine Debatte über die Grundlage des Sozialen.* Frankfurt/ Main: Suhrkamp Verlag, 72-98.

Tyng, Chai M./Amin, Hafeez U./Saad, Mohamad N. M/Malik, Aamir S.(2017): "The Influences of Emotion on Learning and Memory." *Frontiers in Psychology*, 8, 1454.

Verduyn, P., van Mechelen, I., & Tuerlinckx, F. (2011): "The relation between event processing and the duration of emotional experience." *Emotion*, 11, 20–28.

Vyskocilova J., Prasko J. & Slepecky M. (2011): "Empathy in cognitive behavioral therapy and supervision." *Activitas Nervosa Superior Redivia*, 53, 72–83.

Wampold B.E. & Budge S.L. (2012): "The relationship – and its relationship to common and specific factors of psychotherapy." *Society of Counseling Psychology*, 40, 601–623.

Wang C, Schmid CH, Iversen MD, Harvey WF, Fielding RA, Driban JB, Price LL, Wong JB, Reid KF, Rones R, McAlindon T. (2016): "Comparative effectiveness of Tai Chi versus physical therapy for knee osteoarthritis: a randomized trial." *Ann Intern Med,* 165:77-86.

Warneken, Felix, Tomasello, Michael (2008): "Extrinsic Rewards undermine Altruistic Tendencies in 20-Month-Olds." *Developmental Psychology*, 44 (6), 1785-1788.

Warneken, F./Tomasello, M. (2009): "The roots of human altruism." *British Journal of Psychology*, 100: 455-471.

Warren SL, Zhang Y, Duberg K, et al. (2020): "Anxiety and Stress Alter Decision-Making Dynamics and Causal Amygdala-Dorsolateral Prefrontal Cortex Circuits During Emotion Regulation in Children." *Biol Psychiatry*;S0006-3223(20)30100-1.

Watzlawick, Paul, Beavin Bavelas, Janet, Jackson, Don D. (2011): *Pragmatics of Human Communication: A Study of Interactional Patterns, Pathologies and Paradoxes.* New York: W. W. Norton & Company.

Weare, Katherine, Hanh, Thich Nhat (2017): *Happy teachers change the world. A guide for cultivating mindfulness in education*. Berkeley: Parallax Press.

Willutzki, Ulrike, & Teismann, Tobias, Schulte, Dietmar (2012): "Psychotherapy for Social Anxiety Disorder: Long-Term Effectiveness of Resource-Oriented Cognitive-Behavioral Therapy and Cognitive Therapy in Social Anxiety Disorder." *Journal of Clinical Psychology*, 1-11.

Zimmer D. (2000): "Therapiebeendigung – Ideen aus einer kognitiv-behavioralen Perspektive." *Verhaltenstherapie und Verhaltensmedizin*, 21(4), 469-480.

Lightning Source UK Ltd.
Milton Keynes UK
UKHW010636250421
382567UK00001B/10